Intimate Bicycle Tours of Philadelphia

Intimate Bicycle Tours of Philadelphia

Ten Excursions to the City's Art, Parks, and Neighborhoods

PATRICIA VANCE

UNIVERSITY OF PENNSYLVANIA PRESS

Philadelphia

10   9   8   7   6   5   4   3   2   1

Published by
University of Pennsylvania Press
Philadelphia, Pennsylvania 19104-4011

Library of Congress Cataloging-in-Publication Data

Vance, Patricia.
  Intimate bicycle tours of Philadelphia : ten excursions to the city's art, parks, and
neighborhoods / Patricia Vance.
     p.   cm.
  Includes bibliographical references.
  ISBN 0-8122-1868-X (pbk. : alk. paper)
  1. Bicycle touring—Pennsylvania—Philadelphia—Guidebooks. 2. Philadelphia
(Pa.)—Guidebooks. I. Title.
GV1045.5.P42 P558   2004
796.6'2'09748—dc22   2003063361

Contents

Introduction   *1*

TOUR 1   Old City   *9*

TOUR 2   South Philadelphia and Society Hill   *37*

TOUR 3   City Hall and the Parkway   *57*

TOUR 4   Rittenhouse Square and South Broad Street   *80*

TOUR 5   East Fairmount Park   *99*

TOUR 6   West Fairmount Park   *123*

TOUR 7   Germantown and East Mount Airy   *139*

TOUR 8   The Wissahickon Gorge and West Mount Airy   *155*

TOUR 9   Chestnut Hill   *171*

TOUR 10   University City and the Streetcar Suburbs   *185*

For Further Reading   *207*

Introduction

I am a Philadelphia convert. People who convert from one religion to another are often more devout than those who have been members all their lives. It is often the same for people who move to a city from somewhere else. Sometimes the newcomer appreciates the wonderful features that a native resident may take for granted. After living here for twenty years, I love Philadelphia with the zeal of a convert. Philadelphians tend to feel an undeserved inferiority complex about their beautiful city, considering it less urbane than New York, less historic than Boston, and less beautiful than Washington, D.C. Although each of those cities has its own long list of assets, Philadelphia can easily hold its own in comparison. It is a vibrant city with historic sites, thousands of acres of parks, and one of the world's best collections of public art.

In this book's first tour you will visit Old City, often called the most historic square mile in America. The United States was born in the Pennsylvania State House, now called Independence Hall. The Declaration of Independence was signed here and read to the public for the first time in the square just behind the hall. The United States Constitution was debated and signed here. The first members of Congress and the Supreme Court met here. You will see the reconstructed buildings where Thomas Jefferson wrote the Declaration of Independence (Graff House) and where many members of the Continental Congress lodged and met to do business (City Tavern). The nation's first banking center was on Chestnut Street between Second and Fifth Streets. The nation's first library, fire department, art museum, university, public school, horticultural society, and fine arts academy all began in Philadelphia.

In this city with more than three hundred years of history, some older buildings have been preserved while others have been razed to make room for new development. You can sometimes see centuries of history and culture in a single block. Circling the park where the Liberty Bell is located are the eighteenth-century Independence Hall, the Bourse, a nineteenth-century financial office building, and the Rohm and Haas building, erected in 1964. And the pavilion housing the Liberty Bell was constructed in the twenty-first century. This range is not limited to commercial and public buildings. There are twentieth-century town-houses and renovated eighteenth-century row homes within blocks of the national park sites, and new homes are being planned for the future.

Philadelphia has a long, prestigious legacy of architects, from the colonial master builder Robert Smith to the prominent postmodernist Robert Venturi, whose works are discussed in Tours 1 and 9. The neighborhood around Rittenhouse Square (Tour 4) has many beautiful nineteenth-century mansions designed by such notable Victorian architects as Frank Furness and Wilson Eyre. The first American skyscraper built in the International style is in Philadelphia (Tour 3), and the Richards Medical Building, designed by Louis I. Kahn and regarded as one of the country's most important modern buildings, is on the campus of the University of Pennsylvania (Tour 10).

Spanning nearly nine thousand acres, Fairmount Park is the largest city park in the country. It contains formal gardens (the grounds of the Pennsylvania Horticultural Society, Tour 6), ball fields (East Fairmount Park, Tour 5), and natural areas (Wissahickon Gorge, Tour 8). Fairmount Park was established when the city bought up multiple country estates along the Schuylkill River in the mid-1800s, and most of the original estate houses are still owned and maintained by the park and are open to the public.

There is more public art in Philadelphia than in any other city in North America, thanks to the efforts of the Fairmount Park Art Association and the Redevelopment Authority. The art association has spent more than one hundred years accumulating art and installing it throughout the city. The Redevelopment Authority oversees a city ordinance established in 1959 that requires developers to provide public art that is valued at at least 1 percent of their total expenditures. The combined efforts of these two groups have brought more than a thousand works of art to Philadelphia, all of it publicly accessible. There are works by some of the world's greatest artists (Rodin Museum, Tour 5), somber reminders of life's tragedies (*Social Consciousness*, Tour 5), whimsical pieces (*Kangaroos*, Tour 2), memorials to individuals (*George Washington*, Tour 1), and monumental works that have become icons for the city (*Clothespin*, Tour 3). These pieces are supplemented by one of the most impressive collections of mural art in the world, directed by the Department of Recreation's Mural Arts Program. Since 1984, more than two thousand murals have been painted in the city.

Although the city's population continues to decline, the population of the Center City district (Tours 1, 3, and 4) is increasing, and the overall decrease is slowing in several other neighborhoods, including University City (Tour 10) and South Philadelphia (Tour 2). Each year there is more interest in revitalizing the old neighborhoods and more people attend city attractions. Society Hill (Tour 2) is the site of one of America's most successful urban renewal projects. People are attracted to an environment where home is convenient to work and play, and where it is easy to get around by bicycle, on foot, or by public transportation. And there is so much to see and do downtown.

Mark Twain once said that as he grew up, he noticed that his father was getting smarter. Likewise, after years of fleeing to the suburbs, Americans are beginning to appreciate the treasures of our cities. We are looking back to where we've come from, and we are realizing how rich our heritage is and how much our past has in common with the present and the future. To discover those connections, there is no better place than Philadelphia.

WHY A BIKE?

I have traveled by bicycle in many places in the United States and Europe, and I have learned that seeing the sights by bike has many advantages over driving or walking. When you travel by car in any city, the focus is always going to be traffic. It's hard to look at the sculptures or the buildings when you are driving. And sometimes traffic moves too slow or too fast and it's not always easy to pull over when you want a better look. But you can do just that on a bike. You can simply get off a bicycle and move out of traffic onto the sidewalk or the curb. Parking is not a problem; any signpost or fence will do.

You can travel much farther on a bike than on foot. A two-mile walk will take the average person who is looking around most of an hour. But a two-mile bike ride takes ten or fifteen minutes, even for the slowest cyclist. This makes seeing such larger areas as Philadelphia's northwest region easier and more pleasant.

WHAT ARE THE ROUTES LIKE?

All the tours in this book are less than ten miles long. All the routes outside of the northwest are flat. The routes in Center City are the shortest because there is so much to see, not because they are more difficult to ride. Northwest Philadelphia and East and West Fairmount Park (Tours 5–9) can be hilly, but I have tried to find routes that minimize hill climbing.

The routes use paved bike paths or roads with light traffic whenever possible. A few interesting sights are located on busy streets, and I direct you to these places in the safest manner possible. I have given alerts when you need to use extra caution.

An additional advantage that a bike has over a car is that you can hop off the bike, become a pedestrian for a short time, and then hop back on. Throughout these routes I keep this to a minimum; however, there are a couple places where you will need to walk your bike. Sometimes this occurs on a footpath where bicycling is prohibited, and sometimes you will need to walk on the sidewalk for a short time on a one-way street against traffic. There are also a few places where I recommend you walk to avoid dealing with heavy traffic.

In general the routes are simple and easy to follow but, again, the interesting sights don't always cooperate. You will double back a couple times and make some quick turns at other points. You will also make a few small loops. For the best experience, always read ahead so you won't miss the next turn.

WHAT ELSE IS THERE TO DO IN PHILADELPHIA?

In this book I emphasize what you can see by bike, but I also list indoor attractions so that you can stop along the way and visit some of the fine museums, historic buildings, and cultural sites in Philadelphia. Hours of operation are listed along the route, and such additional information as addresses and phone numbers are listed at the end of each tour.

There is so much worth seeing in Philadelphia that it's impossible to include everything in one book, but I hope these rides will show you how much the city has to offer and will encourage you to explore on your own. When you do, you will uncover even more treasures and perhaps you, too, will love Philadelphia with the zeal of the convert.

HOW TO USE THIS BOOK

The ten tours in this book describe ten different routes. I begin each tour with some general information about the route, and I follow this with a brief description of what you will see along the way. Finally, I lay out the route in detail, including the distance from the start and the direction for each turn. Each tour also has a map of the route that shows street names, direction of travel, and sights of interest. When you go touring, after each turn, pause to read both the description of the sights up ahead and the instructions for the next turn.

The general information is arranged in categories as follows:

DISTANCE: All routes are loops that return to the starting point, and all are less than 10 miles (16 km) long. The total distance is given in miles and kilometers.

TERRAIN: I have tried to make the routes easy. However, some have a few challenges that are described in this section. Roads with light traffic and bike paths are used as often as possible, but if you will need to cope with traffic, it will be mentioned. Significant hills and portions of the route that will require you to walk your bike are listed.

START: The starting point of the route is described here.

ACCESS BY CAR: I have provided directions from an interstate highway such as I-76 or I-95. These are not always the most direct or the shortest routes, but they are easy to follow even if you are unfamiliar with the area. This section concludes with suggestions for parking.

ACCESS BY PUBLIC TRANSPORTATION: The Southeastern Pennsylvania Transportation Authority (SEPTA) allows bikes on some of its routes with certain restrictions.

The Broad Street, Market-Frankford, and Norristown High Speed Lines allow bicycles from 9 A.M. to 3 P.M. on weekdays, and on weekends and holidays all day except between 12 A.M. and 5 A.M. You can bring your bike on any car during these times.

Bikes are allowed on all Regional Rail Lines at the same times as the high speed lines, except that bikes are confined to the areas designated for wheelchairs. If a wheelchair-using customer is already on board, the cyclist must wait for the next train.

SEPTA sometimes does not allow more than one nonreserved bicycle per train or car, depending on space available and the mood of the conductor. The maximum allowed without prior approval is five bikes. You can make reservations for groups by calling (215) 580-8403 at least twenty-four hours before your trip. There are no limitations on folding bikes.

SERVICES: In this section I give suggestions on where you can find restaurants. I have also listed places with public restrooms.

BIKE SHOPS: If there are bike shops on the route they are listed here. If there are no bike shops on the route, the closest shop is given. Listings include addresses and phone numbers.

TIPS FOR CYCLISTS

The maps in this book are provided to give you an overview of the route. They are not meant to replace a street map, which you should carry with you. You can get a free Philadelphia Bicycle Map by calling the Philadelphia Streets Department at (215) 686-5560, the Bicycle Coalition of Greater Philadelphia at (215) BICYCLE or (215) 242-9253, the Visitor's Center at (215) 636-1666, or on the Internet at the city's web site, www.phila.gov. The map is excellent for navigation in Center City (Tours 1–4), but you will probably want something more detailed for the other areas of the city. Alfred B. Patton, Inc., makes many detailed maps of the Philadelphia region, available at many bookstores; phone number (215) 345-0700. You will find other choices in local bookstores as well.

Consider food and water before you begin your tours. Each route has some information about places to buy refreshments along the way, but some of the rides are in areas with few stores or restaurants. If possible, always carry a water bottle and a snack. There is much to see in Philadelphia, and you may find that a route will take longer than you expect to complete because you are stopping to take in the sights.

If you stop to visit a site, always securely lock your bike. Choose a sturdy anchored object such as a road sign or fence. Do not, however, block pathways or handrails. Place the lock so that at least the frame is secure. It is best to lock both wheels and the frame if possible.

All bicyclists should be prepared to deal with a flat tire. Carry a patch kit, a spare inner tube of the correct type and size for your bike, and a pump. All these can be purchased inexpensively at any bike shop. If you don't know how to patch a tire or replace an inner tube, consult one of many books on bike repairs. I recommend, among others, *Anybody's Bike Book* by Tom Cuthbertson.

Always obey traffic laws. A bicycle is considered a vehicle in Pennsylvania and is governed by the same laws as cars. If you feel uneasy in a particular situation, you can always get off the bike and onto the sidewalk. You can also walk your bike in crosswalks to get through a difficult intersection. In each tour, areas of the route that have a significant amount of traffic are listed in the **Terrain** section.

ACKNOWLEDGMENTS

Several members of the Bicycle Club of Philadelphia have provided suggestions. I especially want to thank Sid Ozer and Mike McGettigan for their infectious enthusiasm, and the late Bill Ford (it is a Great City and Bill made it a Great Ride). The Germantown Historical Society is wonderful; my special thanks to Jessica Widing, Irvin Miller, and Loretta Witt. And for information on all things about Mount Airy, thank you Patricia Henning. Laura S. Griffith, assistant director of the Fairmount Park Art Association, was generous with her time and knowledge about public art. I hope I have done the art association justice. On a personal level, I received unwavering support from my mother (who is still carrying my first book around with her in case someone she happens to meet on the street hasn't heard about it yet) and my husband Michael Parente (we have fun).

Old City

DISTANCE: 4.0 miles, 6.4 km

TERRAIN: Flat. The route goes along several short walkways. You will need to walk your bike for about 0.5 mile total.

START: Welcome Park on the east side of Second Street between Chestnut and Walnut Streets.

ACCESS BY CAR: From **I-676,** take the Eighth Street exit for Independence Hall. Go south on Eighth Street for three blocks to Market Street. Turn left on Market Street and ride six blocks. Turn right on Second Street. Welcome Park is on the left after one and a half blocks. Park at the meters on the street or at the parking garage on the left at Chestnut Street.

ACCESS BY PUBLIC TRANSPORTATION: All **SEPTA Regional Rail Lines** stop at Market East Station at Filbert and Tenth Streets. Ride south on Tenth Street one block to Market Street. Turn left and ride eight blocks east to Second Street. Turn right. Welcome Park is on the left after one and a half blocks. The **Market/Frankford High Speed Line** stops at Second and Market Streets. Ride one and a half blocks south on Second Street. Welcome Park is on the left. The **Broad Street Subway** stops at City Hall. Ride east on Market Street eleven blocks to Second Street. Turn right. Welcome Park is on the left after one and a half blocks.

SERVICES: There are several places to buy food and drink on Second Street (start of ride and miles 3 to 4). Public restrooms are at Independence Visitor's Center (mile 1.5), Penn's Landing (mile 2.4), and Franklin Court (mile 2.55).

BIKE SHOPS: Trophy Bikes, 311 Market Street (215) 625-7999 (mile

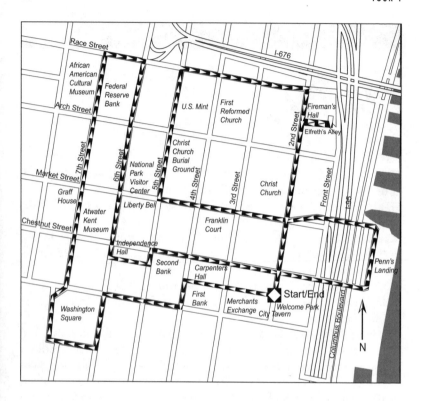

2.5), and **Bike Line,** 1028 Arch Street (215) 923-1310 (not on the route).

One of Philadelphia's mottos is "America starts here," a reference to the city's prominent role in the birth of the United States and as the nation's first capital. The Continental Congress met here, where they drafted and ratified both the Declaration of Independence and the Constitution.

This ride will take you through Old City, where the first colonists built their homes and businesses. Most of Philadelphia's oldest buildings, from the colonial and revolutionary eras and including Independence Hall, are found in Old City, typically defined as the area from Chestnut to Vine Streets and Front to Sixth Streets. This ride stretches the borders a little to the south and west.

Today, Old City looks like it has been lovingly maintained since the eighteenth century, but this section of Philadelphia and much of Society Hill to the south (Tour 2) was neglected for many years. In the 1960s, public and private funds poured into the area for redevelopment.

The ride begins at Welcome Park, located approximately where William Penn lived in 1699 during his second visit to the new colony. During part of the route, you will walk along a few pathways through Independence Park, and wind your way to Washington Square. You will see Independence Hall, as well as a re-creation of the house where Thomas Jefferson wrote the Declaration of Independence, the First and the Second Banks of the United States, the U.S. Mint, and a reconstructed tribute to Philadelphia's favorite son, Benjamin Franklin.

0.0   The ride begins in **Welcome Park** on Second Street between Chestnut and Walnut Streets.

The park commemorates William Penn's Charter of Privileges issued in 1701, guaranteeing freedom of religion and civil liberty to all Philadelphia residents. Penn arrived in the city for the first time in 1682 aboard the ship *Welcome*. He stayed in a house on this site during his second visit, from 1699 to 1701. Created in 1982 to celebrate the three-hun-dred-year anniversary of the founding of Philadelphia, Welcome Park was designed by Venturi, Rauch and Scott Brown. The statue of William Penn is a copy of the one atop City Hall, and the walkway is a replica of Penn's original grid for Philadelphia streets.

The **Thomas Bond House** is the brick building just north of Wel-come Park. Built in 1769 and substantially reconstructed in the twen-tieth century, it was the home of Thomas Bond, a surgeon and a cofounder with Ben Franklin of both Pennsylvania Hospital, the nation's first hospital, and the American Philosophical Society. Today it is a bed-and-breakfast owned by the National Park Service.

This house, like many others you will see, is built of red brick. William Penn and his English contemporaries lived through the Great Fire of London in 1666 when one-third of London's buildings were destroyed, including an estimated 13,000 homes, most of the churches, and many other monumental buildings. This catastrophe influenced the early building materials used in Philadelphia. Brick does not burn and because the soil here was heavy with red clay, red brick was a nat-ural choice.

Across the street at 100 South Second Street you will see the **Cus-toms House,** designed by Ritter and Shay (Tour 3) in 1933. When it was built, there was a gentlemen's agreement that no buildings in Cen-ter City would be taller than the top of Billy Penn's hat on City Hall, resulting in a number of short, squat, not-quite-skyscrapers like this one. The Customs House is a bit out of place among the colonial build-ings in the area, but because of its size it does give you a chance to get a good look at the kind of ornamentation that tops skyscrapers built in the 1920s and 1930s.

Cross Second Street and walk on the footpath to the right of **City Tavern,** a restaurant (open for lunch and dinner) that is a reconstruc-tion of a 1773 tavern frequented by many of the founding fathers, including George Washington and Ben Franklin. John Adams stayed at the original tavern during his service on the Continental Congress. In the city's earliest years, the City Tavern was one of the most popular places to conduct business.

0.05 Continue walking, bearing right along the cobblestones of Dock Street.

The grand marble building slightly to your left at 143 South Third Street is the **Philadelphia Exchange,** also called the **Merchants' Exchange**. It was designed by William Strickland in 1832 and is the oldest stock exchange in America. As Philadelphia's population increased, the taverns were no longer suitable for business transactions and thus the Philadelphia Exchange Company was established. The exchange was dissolved during the Civil War.

The rotunda is unique, but the round tower on top was a copy of the ancient Greek Choragic Monument. Strickland found this design in a pattern book, *Antiquities of Athens* by Stuart and Revett, used extensively by contemporary architects. Strickland's first work as an architect was the Second Bank of the United States, one of the earliest Greek Revival buildings in America. You will see that building later in the tour.

You are following Dock Street now. Dock Street was once Dock Creek, and by the early 1700s it became one of America's first urban blight problems. The creek was often filled with trash and was lined with ramshackle houses. After numerous complaints, the city razed the shacks and filled the creek. The fate of the poor is unknown, but the creek is still here running about eight feet underneath you.

Continue to walk your bike to Third Street.

0.1 Cross Third Street to the First Bank of the United States at 120 South Third Street.

The **First Bank of the United States** was built between 1795 and 1797 in the Roman Revival style by Samuel Blodgett, with major renovations in 1901 by James Windrim. The bank was established by Alexander Hamilton in 1791 to create and control a single currency for the new nation and, perhaps more important, to handle its war debts. A design was chosen that would give the appearance of strength and security, and the bank was one of the most imposing structures built after the Revolution.

The bank's charter was revoked in 1811, and in 1812 businessman Stephen Girard purchased the building as a site for a private bank.

0.15 Continue walking to the left of the bank. After passing the bank, follow the path to the right and then to the left toward the cluster of colonial buildings.

The **New Hall Military Museum** (daily 2–4) and the **National Park Book Store** (daily 9–5) are on the right, and **Carpenters' Hall** (Tu–Su 10–4) is on the left.

Robert Smith built Carpenters' Hall between 1770 and 1774 in the Georgian style. Smith's work formed a large part of the city skyline in colonial times. In addition to Carpenters' Hall, he designed St. Peter's Church and the steeple on Christ Church, both in Philadelphia, the latter probably the most recognized structure in colonial America.

Smith was born in Scotland in 1722 into a family of masons. After an apprenticeship in the building trades, he moved to the colonies in the 1740s and became a member of Philadelphia's Carpenters' Company. Many experts consider Smith to have been the most important master carpenter of Colonial America. Professional architects did not exist as we know them today. A master carpenter was a jack-of-all-trades who knew engineering, masonry, and design and was an active participant in all stages of building.

Smith was also a member of the Philosophical Society and the Continental Congress. During the war, he made wooden boxes with sharp metal-tipped spikes. These were filled with rocks and were sunk in the Delaware to pierce the hulls of British ships. He died in 1777 without witnessing the American victory.

CARPENTERS' HALL, INDEPENDENCE NATIONAL HISTORICAL PARK, FOURTH AND CHESTNUT STREETS

The Carpenters' Company was founded in 1724 and was America's first trade union, modeled after European guilds. In medieval Europe, books were rare and expensive. Knowledge and skills were routes to power and money, and only guild members were allowed access to texts. Sharing information with nonmembers meant expulsion and an end to one's career. There were vast sums of money involved with the construction of such monumental buildings as churches and castles, and membership in a building guild was a guarantee of wealth.

The American colonists were not as wealthy as their European counterparts, but master carpenters were still prosperous and influential, and they guarded their secrets well. The Carpenters' Company published a rule book (for members only) that dictated the price for most of the services a carpenter might perform. Even Thomas Jefferson, as a nonmember, was denied his request for a copy.

After passing in front of Carpenters' Hall, follow the path to the left and then to the right to Fourth Street.

0.2   Left on Fourth Street.

On your left, at the corner just before Walnut Street you will see the **Todd House** at 343 Walnut Street. The house was built in 1775, and lawyer John Todd lived here from 1791 to 1793 with his wife, Dolley Payne Todd. John died in the yellow fever epidemic of 1793, and in 1794 Dolley married Congressman James Madison, who would become the fourth president of the United States. Madison was Secretary of State for Thomas Jefferson and Dolley Madison frequently served as First Lady for the widowed Jefferson as well as for her husband. The garden next to the house is planted as it might have been in the eighteenth century.

0.25   Right on Walnut Street.

Take a look at the **Penn Mutual Life Insurance Company** on the left in the block between Fifth and Sixth Streets. The tall modern building was built in 1969, but the 1838 façade designed by John Haviland was preserved and is the entrance to a courtyard in front of the new building.

Haviland was trained as an architect in England and became one of the first professional architects in America. He wrote *The Builder's Assistant*, the first American pattern book, and he taught at the Franklin Institute, which he also designed. Today that building houses the Atwater Kent Museum, also on this tour.

Haviland also designed Eastern State Penitentiary in Philadelphia (Tour 3) and prisons in New York City, Missouri, Rhode Island, and Arkansas. He also designed the Walnut Street Theatre (Tour 4).

0.45 Left on Sixth Street.

You will now ride around the perimeter of **Washington Square**, one of William Penn's five original squares.

Washington Square was used as a pasture by local farmers and as a graveyard for itinerants as well as the city's poor from 1704 to 1794. Bodies were buried in canvas without coffins or permanent markers. Many African Americans buried their dead here and conducted funerals and ceremonies to honor them.

The Walnut Street Jail was located at Sixth and Walnut Streets from 1775 to 1835. This was the site of incredible cruelty to both American and British soldiers during the Revolution. The British occupied Philadelphia in the winter of 1777 and kept prisoners of war here, frequently depriving them of food and blankets. Most prisoners did not survive the winter. Their bodies were placed in oak coffins and piled on top of one another in twenty-by-thirty-foot pits along Seventh and Walnut Streets. After the Americans regained the city, they used the jail for British prisoners, who fared no better than the Americans and whose bodies were also dumped into trenches. The yellow fever epidemic of 1793 saw another surge of burials in the square before it was closed as a graveyard the next year.

After 1790, the Pennsylvania Assembly passed a series of bills that made this jail the site of the earliest experiments in prison reform in the United States. The laws called for separation of men and women, juveniles and adults, and debtors and felons. The jail also provided rehabilitation for inmates. Prisoners could work off the cost of their incarceration while learning a marketable trade from skilled artisans.

Recidivism among those who participated was significantly lower than among those who did not.

One of the most famous of this jail's debtors was Robert Morris, who provided funding for the Revolution. George Washington visited him many times.

The square was surrounded by a shantytown for the poor until 1815, when the city began an effort to improve the area. Washington Square now boasts more than sixty varieties of trees, the result of a project begun in 1816. In 1825, the square was sufficiently genteel to be deemed worthy of bearing the name of the young country's first president.

The **Tomb of the Unknown Soldier** was erected in 1954 to memorialize the soldiers buried here. An archaeological team unearthed a Continental soldier's body for entombment in the memorial, now located in the center of the square. The exact location of the burial trenches was not known, and many pilot holes were needed to locate a suitable skeleton. An oak coffin was unearthed that contained the remains of a twenty-year-old male with a head wound that could have been caused by a musket ball. It is possible, however, that this is the body of a British soldier. Nonetheless, an inscription on the monument reads, "Beneath this stone rests a soldier of Washington's army who died to give you liberty."

A statue of **George Washington** stands in the middle of the tomb. In 1791 Jean-Antoine Houdon sculpted the marble original, now located in the Virginia State House. This bronze casting was made in 1922.

The first balloon flight in America took place here on January 9, 1793. With most of Philadelphia's prominent citizens in attendance, including President Washington, French aeronaut Jean-Pierre Blanchard lifted up from the jail yard. The balloon floated over the Delaware River and landed in Gloucester, New Jersey. Several members of the crowd followed the flight on their horses and carried the aeronaut back to cheering crowds.

Less than a hundred yards from the balloon lift-off site you'll see a **sycamore tree.** This tree was planted in 1975 from seed carried to the moon on Apollo 14 by astronaut Stuart Roosa.

The **Athenaeum of Philadelphia** (M, Tu, Th, F 9–5, W 12–8) is on the east side of the square at 219 South Sixth Street. It was designed in 1845 by John Notman (Tour 4). The Athenaeum was founded in 1814 as a social and literary club for young men and was named after the Greek goddess of wisdom. There were many other Athenaeums in other cities in America.

0.55 Right on South Washington Square.

Washington Square has been the home of many major publishers in the last century or so. The **Lea and Febiger building** at 600 South Washington Square was founded in 1758 by Mathew Carey and is the oldest publishing house in the country.

0.65 Right on West Washington Square.

The **Farm Journal Building** was erected in 1911 and is in the southwest corner, with a stone cornucopia over the door. The *Journal* was first published in 1827 and was aimed at farmers who lived within a day's buggy ride of Philadelphia. Today it is the largest farming magazine in the country.

The old headquarters of **W. B. Saunders Publishing Company** is on the corner of Locust and Seventh Streets. Saunders publishes medical texts, the most famous of which is probably the 1948 groundbreaking *Kinsey Report,* the first scientific treatise on American sexual practices.

A bit to the north you will see a building with a pair of bronze doors, flanked by two art deco sculptures. Ralph Becker built the building in 1928 for **N. W. Ayer and Sons**, which was founded in 1869 and is the country's oldest advertising company.

Continue riding north on Seventh Street.

The Italianate building on the corner at 700–710 Walnut Street was the headquarters of the **Philadelphia Savings Fund Society (PSFS)**, founded in 1816. The building was completed in 1869.

0.75 Bear right and then go straight across Walnut Street on Seventh Street.

The **Atwater Kent Museum** (W–M 10–4), on the right at 15 South Seventh Street, is the official museum of Philadelphia's history. The building was the original location of the Franklin Institute in 1825 and was designed by John Haviland after the Greek monument of Thrasyllus. The Franklin Institute was founded by Samuel Merrick to promote research, communication, and education in the sciences. Haviland, William Strickland, and Thomas U. Walter taught architecture here. The Franklin Institute relocated in 1933 to its current location on the Franklin Parkway, and this building was almost demolished. Fortunately, in 1938 an inventor and manufacturer, A. Atwater Kent, established a museum of Philadelphia history here.

The **Declaration House** (daily 10–1), a reconstruction of Jacob Graff, Jr.'s, house, where Jefferson wrote the Declaration of Independence, is on the left side of Seventh Street just before Market Street. The original Georgian building, constructed in 1775, was razed in 1883. The $2 million reconstruction in 1975 was part of the massive renewal of the Independence Mall area.

After two blocks the **African American Museum in Philadelphia** (Tu–Sa 10–5, Su 12–6) is on the left on the northwest corner of Seventh and Arch Streets. It was founded in 1976 and is dedicated to the culture of African Americans.

The sculpture in front of the museum is *Nesaika* by John Rhoden, installed when the museum opened. The style is African but the name means "we" or "our" in Chinook Indian language. Rhoden sought to highlight the diversity of the American heritage.

1.3   Right on Race Street.

Independence Mall starts here and extends south to Chestnut Street.

1.35   Right on Sixth Street.

The **Federal Reserve Bank** is at 100 North Sixth Street at Arch Street. It was constructed between 1973 and 1976, and it houses offices for the Federal Reserve as well as special facilities for handling currency. There is a vault the length of a football field that holds millions of dollars.

Phaedrus, a sculpture created by Beverly Pepper in 1967, is in front of the bank. The artist designed the work to appear to be delicately balanced, as life itself is. This is one example of the public art created as part of Philadelphia's 1-percent ordinance. In 1959, the Philadelphia City Council enacted legislation requiring developers to contribute public art valuing 1 percent of the total development costs. Combined with the efforts of the Fairmount Park Art Association, the ordinance has endowed the city with more than one thousand works of public art, more than any other city in North America.

Between Arch and Market Streets, in front of the **Federal Courthouse,** you can see the unusual fountain *Voyage of Ulysses* by David von Schlegell, installed in 1977. Von Schlegell worked as an aviation engineer and used the assistance of hydraulic engineers to create the fountain's effect.

The sculpture *Bicentennial Dawn* by Louise Nevelson is inside the courthouse but visible from the courtyard. It is a collection of white wooden columns that are carved in intricate abstract patterns. Many art historians consider Nevelson to be the first woman to achieve international acclaim as a sculptor.

The **Independence Visitor Center** (daily 8:30–5) is on the left at Sixth and Market Streets. This is where you can get information about reservations and tickets for tours of Independence Hall and other buildings in the national park.

The new **Liberty Bell Center** (daily 9–5) opened in October 2003 on Sixth Street between Market and Chestnut Streets. A procession attended by thousands of people took four hours to move the American icon, connected to sensitive motion detectors, some 300 feet from its old location facing Market Street. The bell was cast in England and brought here to celebrate the fiftieth anniversary of William Penn's Charter of Privileges, which guaranteed freedom of religion to all Pennsylvania residents. The bell cracked in transit or shortly after arrival and was melted and recast locally. It was mounted in the steeple of the State House, now Independence Hall, and rung for special occasions. By 1774, the steeple was in such poor condition that the bell was not used for fear that the steeple would collapse. Tradition has it, however, that the bell was rung to bring Philadelphians to the State House to hear the Declaration of Independence read for the first time. Whether or not the Liberty Bell rang, certainly many others in the area did and the Liberty Bell became an important symbol. The bell was removed from the steeple and hidden from the British when they captured the city in the winter of 1777 for fear they would destroy it. It cracked again in the nineteenth century and was rung for the last time in 1846 on Washington's birthday.

The **Rohm and Haas Building** on Sixth Street, just south of Market Street, was erected in 1964. The Rohm and Haas Corporation, the first private investor to develop property on Independence Mall, chose modern designs to contrast with the Georgian style of the Colonial buildings. Rohm and Haas are manufacturers of Plexiglas, which they put to good use especially in the lighting fixtures, visible from the sidewalk and were designed by Bauhaus designer, Gyory Kepes.

Milkweed Pod is a fountain in the courtyard in the middle of the building but is visible from the street. It was created by Clark B. Fitzgerald in 1965 as the Rohm and Haas public art contribution.

On Sixth Street, just south of Chestnut Street, is the **Public Ledger Building**, built by Horace Trumbauer in 1924. Philadelphia's first penny journal, the *Ledger*, was founded by Cyrus H. K. Curtis in 1836 and was the city's leading newspaper until 1940. The Curtis Center is up ahead on the corner. The Public Ledger Building was erected in the elaborate Georgian Revival style typical of Trumbauer, who also designed the Philadelphia Museum of Art.

The **PECO Energy Liberty Center** is in the Public Ledger Building on the corner of Sixth and Sansom Streets, facing Sansom. This is the starting point of the Lights of Liberty, a dramatic evening light show and history lesson that takes you to six locations around Old City, ending back at the PECO center.

The **Curtis Center** (M–F 9–5, Sa 8–1) is the next building. Erected in 1916, it is the former home of Curtis Publishing Company, which became one of the country's largest publishing houses and produced the *Saturday Evening Post*. Today it is an office complex. There is a twelve-story atrium, and the marble lobby holds the spectacular Louis Comfort Tiffany glass mosaic *The Dream Garden*, based on a painting by Maxfield Parrish. The mural is fifteen by forty-nine feet and was constructed from 1914 to 1916 using more than 100,000 pieces of glass in 266 colors. The Curtis family attempted to sell the mosaic in the 1990s, but public outcry prompted the city to wage a battle to keep the mosaic here. After much litigation, it seems the work will remain where it is. The building is open to the public during normal business hours and the mosaic is definitely worth a stop.

1.8   Left at Sansom Street. Dismount your bike and use the walkway through **Independence Square** with Independence Hall on your left.

The Pennsylvania State House, now called **Independence Hall** (daily 9–5), was constructed at least between 1734 and 1748. Some sources say it was started as early as 1731; others give the completion date as late as 1754. Designers Andrew Hamilton and Edmund Wooley used the work of British architect Christopher Wren as inspiration. Andrew Hamilton, a lawyer, had traveled to England and had many books on English architecture. Wooley was a master carpenter and member of the Carpenters' Company. The building has been renovated many times over the years but was restored to its 1776 appearance by the National Park Service in 1950.

Independence Hall is where America was born. The Second Continental Congress met here from 1775 to 1783, the Declaration of Independence was ratified in 1776, the Articles of Confederation were adopted in 1781, and the Constitution of the United States was debated, written, and signed in 1787. The Declaration was read in public for the first time in Independence Square, and George Washington was appointed commander-in-chief of the Continental Army here.

The British Army captured Philadelphia in late 1777, and the troops destroyed many of the original furnishings, but the park service has replaced those pieces with others from the same period.

The building has often served as an American icon. President-elect Lincoln raised a new United States flag with thirty-four stars here after Kansas joined the Union following a bloody battle over slavery. Four years later, his body was laid in state here as thousands passed to mourn.

Congress Hall (daily 2–5), west of Independence Hall, dates to

1787–1789. To the east is **Old City Hall** (daily 2–5), home of the U.S. Supreme Court in 1790 and 1791. This building became Philadelphia's City Hall when the federal government moved to Washington, D.C. City government remained here until 1901, when the current City Hall was completed.

Independence Hall is in the Georgian style while Congress Hall and Old City Hall are Federal. After the Revolutionary War, Americans were eager to gain artistic as well as political independence from England, and the Georgian style (named for the four Kings George) was modified and renamed Federal in honor of the new government. Both styles use decorative elements from ancient Greece and Rome, and both are rigidly symmetrical. Federal buildings, however, have larger windows with fewer panes of glass and higher ceilings and are lighter and airier.

From this side of Independence Hall you can see the Palladian window, a three-part style popular in both Federal and Georgian architecture. The central arched window is flanked by two square-topped windows.

Philosophical Hall (April–Sept., W–Su 12–5; Oct.–March, Th–Su 12–5) is next to Old City Hall and was constructed from 1785 to 1789. The American Philosophical Society was founded by Ben Franklin to facilitate the dissemination of knowledge. In January 2003, Philosophical Hall was open to the public for the first time in almost two hundred years, displaying colonial era scientific instruments, prints and manuscripts. Across Fifth Street is **Library Hall** (M–F 9–5), built in 1954 on the site of the Library Company of Philadelphia, which was also founded by the truly industrious Ben Franklin. The original building was demolished in 1888.

1.9 Turn left and ride north on Fifth Street.

Before you turn onto Chestnut Street, look to the left in front of Independence Hall. You'll see a bronze casting of a sculpture of **George**

☞ **INDEPENDENCE HALL, INDEPENDENCE NATIONAL HISTORICAL PARK, FOURTH AND CHESTNUT STREETS**

Washington. Joseph Alexis Bailly created the original marble sculpture in 1869 and the cast was made in 1908. Bailly was born in France, the son of a cabinetmaker. He fled France after apparently shooting his commanding officer during the 1848 uprising. He joined the faculty of the Pennsylvania Academy of the Fine Arts in 1850. The original marble sculpture was installed here in 1869 but was moved to City Hall in 1908 to protect it from the weather.

1.95 Right on Chestnut Street.

Pass the sculpture *The Signer* by Evangelos Frudakis. Installed in 1980, it is a tribute to the monumental documents signed in Independence Hall during the eighteenth century.

The **Second Bank of the United States** (daily 10–3) is on the right at 420 Chestnut Street. It was built in 1818–1824 by William Strickland, whose Merchants' Exchange Building you have already seen on this tour.

Strickland was one of nineteenth-century America's most influential architects. He apprenticed for Benjamin Latrobe, who designed America's first Greek Revival building in Philadelphia. The Second Bank was Strickland's first building, and although Latrobe's building predates it by twenty years, it was the Second Bank that started the Greek Revival movement that swept the country in the first half of the nineteenth century. America was eager to build a culture separate from Europe, yet ironically the first truly American architectural style was a revival of an ancient Greek design. Americans idealized the ancient Greek democracy and felt a kinship with the modern Greeks because of their war of independence against Turkey in the early nineteenth century. The exterior of the Second Bank is modeled on the Greek Parthenon; it was intended to give air of security, wealth, and history.

The Second Bank was formed by the federal government in 1816 after the charter of the First Bank was revoked. In 1836, protest over the lack of credit available for small businesses and farmers forced President Andrew Jackson to veto the renewal of the Second Bank's charter, creating financial panic that led to the country's first depression. The Second Bank failed and Strickland remodeled it into the Cus-

**SECOND BANK OF THE UNITED STATES, INDEPENDENCE NATIONAL HISTORI-
CAL PARK, FOURTH AND CHESTNUT STREETS**

toms House in 1840. Today the building houses a collection of portraits of Revolutionary War–era Americans.

Revocation of the bank's charter created a dramatic rise in commercial banking. In Philadelphia, banks were built near the center of local
government, which was still at Independence Square. Chestnut Street
from Third to Fifth Streets became known as Bank Row. At the time,
the Italian Renaissance Revival style was favored for banks; it was
thought to give the appearance of wealth. This style features rectangu-
lar, boxy buildings with many ornamental details. One distinctive ele-
ment is a heavy overhanging cornice with carved supporting brackets.
Doors, entrances, and window frames were often made of intricately
carved wood or stone.

**Pennsylvania Company for Insurances on Lives and Granting Annu-
ities,** built from 1871 to 1873, is across the street at 431 Chestnut

Street. Next door is the **Farmers' and Mechanics' Bank** at 427 Chestnut Street, built in 1854–55 and renovated in 1984 and 1993. Third is the **Bank of Pennsylvania,** at 421 Chestnut Street, also in Italian Renaissance style but more highly ornamented, auguring later Victorian decorative excesses. There was a panic and a run on banks in 1857, and this one didn't survive. The half-finished building was purchased and completed by the Philadelphia Bank. Between Fourth and Third Streets on the north side of Chestnut Street, Bank Row continues. **Philadelphia National Bank** at 323 Chestnut Street was erected in 1898.

Next is the **National Liberty Museum** (Tu–Sa 10–4:30, Su 12–4) at 321 Chestnut Street, honoring the sacrifices made by individuals to preserve liberty for others. Exhibits combine powerful accounts of personal heroism with stunning works of art in glass, including *The Flame of Liberty,* a twenty-foot-high sculpture by Dale Chihuly. The museum chose the medium of glass to represent the fragility of life. The approach is a wonderful counterpoint to the more typical exhibitions in the area.

Continuing east, the **First National Bank** is at 315 Chestnut Street. John McArthur, Jr., designed this bank and then went on to work on City Hall (Tour 3).

In the mid-nineteenth century, in the migration pattern that still exists today, Philadelphians began moving their residences to the west. As this occurred, the block between Third and Second Streets on Chestnut began to attract warehouse developers. In 1854, Joseph C. Hoxie built the Elliott and Leland Building in commercial Italianate style on the left at 235 to 237 Chestnut Street.

Also on the left on the northeast corner of Second Street is the **Corn Exchange**, built in 1900. Unlike its Italianate neighbors, the style is Georgian Revival with baroque stone carvings.

On the road itself, note that there are Belgian blocks on Chestnut Street between Second and Front Streets. These can make rough riding and you may wish to walk your bike for this block.

2.35 Cross over I-95 on the bridge to Penn's Landing.

2.4 Left at **Penn's Landing.**

This is the approximate site of William Penn's arrival in 1682, although at that time the river ran next to Front Street, and this area would have been underwater. Revival of the seaport began in 1967. Among the attractions are **Independence Seaport Museum** (daily 10–5), Admiral Dewey's 1892 cruiser *Olympia,* a World War II–era submarine, and an active wooden boat workshop.

2.55 Left on Market Street.

Franklin Court (daily 10–5) is on the left at 312–322 Market Street. Robert Smith designed a house for Ben Franklin in a courtyard on this site in 1763. Two years later, Franklin's wife, Deborah, moved in while he was in England. When Franklin returned to Philadelphia, he joined her here until his death in 1790 at the age of eighty-four. His daughter Sarah Bache then inherited the house and lived here until her death in 1808. Bache's heirs sold the house and it was demolished in 1812.

Franklin also owned three rental properties on **Market Street at 316, 318, and 320** (daily 10–5). These were also demolished but were rebuilt in the late 1900s. Today, there is a print shop similar to Franklin's in 320, an architectural exhibit of the area in 318, and 316 is a U.S. Post Office decorated in eighteenth-century fashion. There is also an underground museum (daily 2–5) devoted to Franklin.

Archaeology of this site began in 1953. Although many artifacts and outbuildings were found, there was nothing left of Franklin's home except the foundations. With insufficient information to reconstruct the house, the National Park Service took a different route to creating a park dedicated to Franklin. Prominent architects Robert Venturi and John Rauch designed *Ghost Structure* to evoke the feeling of the house without attempting to reproduce it. You can see it by passing through the archway on Market Street into the brick courtyard.

Ben Franklin came to Philadelphia in 1723 at the age of seventeen. He married Deborah Read, whom he met the first day he arrived. By the time of the American Revolution, Franklin was, and continues to be, Philadelphia's most famous resident. He published the *Pennsylva-*

nia Gazette and *Poor Richard's Almanac*, and he was Pennsylvania Assembly Public Printer, Pennsylvania Postmaster, Justice of the Peace, and Clerk of the Pennsylvania Assembly. He founded or helped found numerous organizations including the American Philosophical Society, the University of Pennsylvania, Pennsylvania Hospital, the Library Company, and the Philadelphia Contributionship, America's first fire department. He represented America in both England and France, and he invented the Franklin stove, bifocals, and the lightning rod. He coined the phrases "A penny saved is a penny earned" and "Beer is proof that God loves us and wants us to be happy." His likeness was everywhere during his lifetime, and it continues to surround us in Philadelphia today. And this is not the last you will hear of him on this tour.

But for now, continue on Market Street. The sculpture *Gift of the Winds* by Joseph C. Bailey was created as a public art offering in 1978 and stands at Fifth and Market Streets on the right.

2.95 Right on Fifth Street.

The **National Museum of American Jewish History** (M–Th 10–5, F 10–3, Su 12–5) is around the corner at 55 North Fifth Street. The museum is dedicated to the history of the American Jewish experience. In 2002 the museum began extensive renovations expected to be completed in 2006. Only a small gallery with information about the new building is now open, but you can visit Congregation Mikveh Israel, which is part of the museum. It was founded in 1740 and is the oldest Jewish congregation in Philadelphia and the second oldest in the country (Tour 2).

Religious Liberty, a sculpture created by Moses Jacob Ezekiel in 1876, is in front of the museum. It was exhibited in Rome before it arrived in Philadelphia for the national centennial in 1876. Originally located in Fairmount Park, it was moved here in 1984.

The **Free Quaker Meeting House** is on the left on Fifth Street just before Arch Street. It was constructed and founded as a meeting house in 1783 by a group of Quakers who took exception to the traditional Quaker opposition to war during the American Revolution. It served as a meeting house for some two hundred Quakers who believed that it was morally correct to fight what they believed was an immoral government. Over the years, members returned to other meeting houses, and in 1834 this meeting house was closed.

Christ Church Burial Grounds are on the right opposite the Free Quaker Meeting House at the corner of Arch Street. The graves of seven signers of the Declaration of Independence, including Benjamin Franklin, are here. Franklin's grave is visible through the fence on Arch Street, a short distance from the corner of Fifth Street.

On the other side of Arch Street is the **United States Mint,** with the capacity to make thirty-two million coins per day. This building is the fourth in Philadelphia to be home to the U.S. Mint. America's first mint, built in 1792, was located about two blocks from here. George Washington was so eager to see the mint succeed that he donated his personal silver possessions to be used for America's first coins. When the federal government moved to Washington, D.C., it was decided to continue the Philadelphia mint since it was fully operational and the moving cost would be enormous. Tours are by reservation only.

3.25 Right on Race Street.

The **Police Administration Building,** constructed in 1967, is on Race Street to your left between Seventh and Eighth Streets. It consists of two circles connected by an arch, providing efficient use of floor space and an unusual appearance.

From here you have a great view of the **Benjamin Franklin Bridge** and the sculpture *Bolt of Lightning . . . A Memorial to Benjamin Franklin.* The bridge was built in 1926 and designed by Paul Philippe Cret, who also designed the Franklin Parkway. Isamu Noguchi conceived the sculpture in 1933, but it wasn't installed until 1984.

Just past Fourth Street on Race is the **Old First Reformed United Church of Christ** (M–F 8:30–3), founded by German settlers in 1727. The present building is the third built here and was erected in 1837. The congregation moved from this location in 1882, and the building was used as a warehouse until 1966, when it was restored.

3.45 Right on Second Street.

The **Fireman's Hall Museum** (Tu–Sa 9–4:30) is on the left at the next corner, Quarry Street. This restored 1900 firehouse has displays on the history of fire fighting in America. Early fire-fighting equipment in the museum includes hand-drawn, horse-drawn, and steam-powered equipment as well as an impressive collection of fire marks, plaques that hung on the homes of people who subscribed to a fire company. If you had a fire mark, you could count on the assistance of that fire company.

The first floor contains a poignant exhibit about New York fire-fighters who lost their lives on September 11, 2001, and several vintage fire-fighting vehicles. The second floor includes re-creations of early living quarters of firefighters. The first fire company in this country was started by none other than Ben Franklin.

3.55 Left on **Elfreth's Alley**.

This collection of thirty colonial and post-colonial houses is known as the oldest continuously occupied street in the United States. Its history begins around 1700; the Delaware River ran along Front Street, and this alley was used to haul cargo to and from the ships. Shortly thereafter, blacksmith Arthur Wells and bolter John Gilbert built their homes here. The omnipresent Ben Franklin lived here immediately after he arrived in Philadelphia. The oldest homes may be numbers 122 and 124, dating to 1725 and 1727. Numbers 124 and 126 are museums (Mar–Dec Tu–Sa 10–4, Su 12–4; Jan–Feb Sa–Su 12-4), but the rest of the houses are private residences.

3.6 Turn around at the end of Elfreth's Alley and return to Second Street.

3.65 Left on Second Street.

The **Tuttleman Brothers and Fagen Building** is on the right between Arch and Church Streets at 56 to 60 North Second Street. Built out of brick from 1830 to 1836, it was renovated in 1900 with what was probably the last cast-iron façade erected in America. It became one of

ELFRETH'S ALLEY HISTORIC DISTRICT, SECOND STREET BETWEEN RACE AND ARCH STREETS

the first buildings in the city renovated for loft apartments during the 1970s.

Christ Church (Episcopal) (daily 9–5) on the right just after Church Street is one of Philadelphia's treasures. It was erected between 1727 and 1754, replacing an earlier wooden church built in 1697. It was originally called the Nation's Church after the American Revolution. Dr. John Kearlsey supervised construction of the main section and Robert Smith built the steeple. The brick section of the steeple was erected quickly but there wasn't enough money to finish the wooden top. Our boy Franklin organized three lotteries to raise the necessary funds. In 1789, American members of the Church of England organized the Protestant Episcopal Church of the United States here, and today it remains an active Episcopal church.

4.0   End your tour back at **Welcome Park**.

ATTRACTIONS IN OLD CITY

African American Museum in Philadelphia, 701 Arch Street (215) 547-0380, Tu–Sa 10–5, Su 12–6, http://www.aampmuseum.org, admission.

Athenaeum of Philadelphia, 219 South Sixth Street (215) 925-2688, M, Tu, Th, F 9–5, W 12–8, http://www.libertynet.org/~athena, free.

Atwater Kent Museum, 15 South Seventh Street (215) 685-4830, W–M 10–4, http://www.philadelphiahistory.org, admission.

Christ Church (Episcopal), 20 North American Street (215) 922-1695, daily 9–5, free.

Christ Church Burial Grounds, southeast corner of Fifth and Arch Streets (215) 922-1695, call ahead for access.

Curtis Center, Sixth and Walnut Streets (215) 238-6450, M–F 9–5, Sa 8–1, free.

Elfreth's Alley, house museums at 124 and 126 (215) 574-0560, March–Dec., Tu–Sa 10–4, Su 12–4; Jan.–Feb., Sa–Su 12–4, http://www.elfrethsalley.org, admission.

Fireman's Hall Museum, 147 North Second Street (215) 923-1438, Tu–Sa 9–4:30, http://www.angelfire.com/pa4/firemanshall, free.

First Friday. Forty art galleries in Old City participate; most are between Second and Third, Market and Race (800) 555-5191, first Friday of each month, 5–9. Many galleries are also open on Wednesday evenings, http://www.oldcity.org/ocaanew/group.html, free.

Independence National Historic Park (215) 597-8974, fax (215) 597-0042, daily 9–5 unless otherwise noted, http://www.nps.gov/inde.html, free unless otherwise noted.

> America's National Parks Museum Shop, Chestnut Street between Third and Fourth Streets
>
> Carpenters' Hall, 320 Chestnut Street (215) 925-0167, Tu–Su 10–4
>
> City Tavern, daily, opens at 11:30, serves lunch and dinner
>
> Congress Hall, Sixth and Chestnut Streets, daily 2–5
>
> Declaration House, Market and Seventh Streets, daily 12–2
>
> Franklin Court, 321-322 Market Street, daily 2-5
> > Fragments of Franklin Court, temporarily closed
> > Museum Shop, daily 9–4:30
> > Printing Office
> > Underground Museum
> > U.S. Post Office and Postal Museum
>
> Independence Hall, Chestnut Street between Fifth and Sixth Streets
>
> Independence Visitors Center, Sixth and Market Streets, daily 8:30–5, July 1–Sept. 1 daily 8:30–6
>
> Liberty Bell Center, Market Street between Fifth and Sixth Streets
>
> Library Hall, Fifth Street between Chestnut and Walnut Streets, M–F 9–5

New Hall Military Museum, Chestnut Street between Third and Fourth Streets, daily 2–5

Old City Hall, Fifth and Chestnut Streets, daily 10–1,

Philosophical Hall, Fifth Street between Chestnut and Walnut Streets, April–Sept., W–Su 12–5; Oct.–March, Th–Su 12–5

Second Bank of the United States, temporarily closed

Todd and Bishop White House Tours, free tour tickets required, available at the visitors center

Independence Seaport Museum, Penn's Landing at Walnut Street, 211 South Columbus Boulevard (215) 925-5439, daily 10–5, http://seaport.philly.com, admission.

Lights of Liberty, PECO Energy Liberty Center, Sixth and Chestnut Streets, (877) 452-1776, call for times, www.lightsofliberty.org, admission.

National Museum of American Jewish History and Congregation Mikveh Israel, 55 North Fifth Street (215) 923-3811, fax (215) 923-0763, M–Th 10–5, F 10–3, Su 12–5, http://www.nmajh.org, admission not charged until the new building opens in 2006.

National Liberty Museum, 321 Chestnut Street (215) 925-2800, Tu–Sa 10–4:30, Su 12–4, www.libertymuseum.org, admission.

Old First Reformed United Church of Christ, southeast corner of Fourth and Race Streets (215) 922-4566, M–F 8:30–3, tours by appointment, services Su 11, free.

Penn's Landing, Columbus Boulevard from Market to South Streets. Walking bridges at Market, Chestnut, Walnut, and South Streets (215) 922-2386, daily dawn to dusk, http://www.pennslandingcorp.com, free.

Thomas Bond House, Second Street, open all year, http://www.winston-salem-inn.com/philadelphia

South Philadelphia and Society Hill

DISTANCE: 6.0 miles, 9.7 km

TERRAIN: Flat. There are two sections where you will need to walk your bike; each is less than 0.1 mile.

START: Gloria Dei, or Old Swedes', Church on Christian Street between Swanson and Water Streets, one block west of Columbus Boulevard.

ACCESS BY CAR: Take **I-95** to the Columbus Boulevard/Washington Avenue exit. From northbound I-95, go left onto Columbus Boulevard, and left onto Christian Street. From southbound I-95, go right onto Columbus Boulevard, and right onto Christian Street. Gloria Dei is on the left. There is on-street parking in the immediate area.

ACCESS BY PUBLIC TRANSPORTATION: All **SEPTA Regional Rail Lines** stop at Market East Station at Tenth and Filbert Streets. Ride south on Tenth Street approximately one mile to Christian Street. Turn left. Ride east approximately one mile to Gloria Dei, on the right just after Water Street. The **Market/Frankford High Speed Line** stops at Second and Market Streets. Ride south on Second Street. Just after Walnut Street, bear left where the name changes to Dock Street. Turn right at the "T" at Spruce Street and immediately turn left to return to Second Street. Left on Christian Street in about 1 mile. Take the Lombard/South exit from the **Broad Street Subway.** Ride east on South Street for twelve blocks. Turn right on Second Street. After about 0.5 mile turn left on Christian Street. Gloria Dei is on the right in two blocks at Water Street.

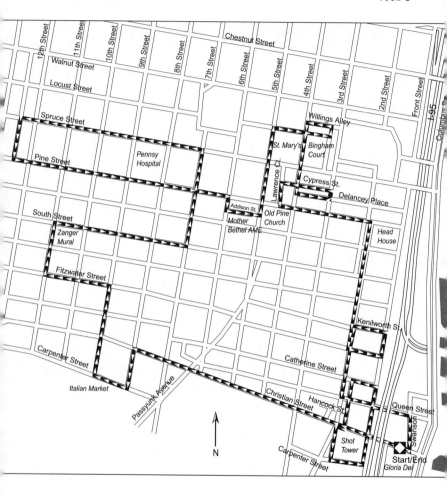

SERVICES: Restaurants in the Italian Market at Ninth and Christian Streets (mile 1.5) and on South Street (mile 2.0 to 2.3 and 5.0).

BIKE SHOPS: Village Bikes, 792 South Second Street (215) 629-4141 (mile 1.5), and **Via Bikes,** 606 South Ninth Street (215) 627-3370 (mile 5.3).

South Philadelphia is sort of a super-neighborhood encompassing many smaller areas, each with its own distinctive feel. You won't see all of South Philly on this route, but you'll experience a few of its niches. As you ride through these neighborhoods you will see modern residences and colonial houses side by side in a living community.

The ride begins in Queen Village, also known as Southwark, the oldest neighborhood in Philadelphia. The first colonists in Queen Village were Swedish immigrants who arrived before William Penn's surveyors and named the area for Sweden's Queen Christina. Next you'll pay a visit to the Italian Market, the oldest and largest outdoor market in the country. The route will also take you to Mother Bethel African Methodist Episcopal (AME) Church founded in 1787 by former slave Richard Allen, who is buried in a tomb beneath the church. You will pass through Society Hill, one of America's most successful urban renewal projects, before returning to Queen Village.

0.0   Begin at **Gloria Dei,** or **Old Swedes', Church** (daily 9–5), at the corner of Water Street and Christian Street.

This peaceful and charming place is incongruously located next to the elevated interstate highway. You will forget the rush and noise, however, as soon as you step into the cemetery, one of Philadelphia's oldest, with tombstones from the early 1700s. Several Revolutionary War soldiers are buried here, including Captain George Ord, who stole gunpowder from the British for the Continental Army.

Built in 1698 to replace an earlier log cabin, Gloria Dei is the second oldest Swedish church in the United States and the oldest church in

Pennsylvania. It has been in continuous use since that time and may be the only seventeenth-century building in Philadelphia that would be recognized by the people who built it. Today it is an Episcopal church.

Betsy Ross was married in this church. Born Elizabeth Griscom, she was denounced by the Society of Friends in 1774 when she eloped with John Ross, a member of the Church of England. Ross owned an upholstery shop on Arch Street, and Betsy took over the business when John died in 1776 in an explosion while serving with the militia.

The story of George Washington and members of the Continental Congress arriving in Betsy Ross's shop to commission the first American flag is almost certainly fiction. George Washington was in New York when the meeting was supposed to have taken place, and the "Stars and Stripes" was not accepted as America's official flag until after the Revolution. Betsy Ross did make flags, among other items, and George Washington and several other prominent leaders of the Revolution attended her wedding to Joseph Ashburn here at Gloria Dei in 1777.

Ashburn was captured by the British while serving on an American ship and died a prisoner of war, leaving Betsy widowed once more, this time with two young children. In 1783 she married John Claypoole, who had been in prison with Ashburn. The Claypooles had five daughters and were married more than thirty years. He died in 1817, twenty years before his wife.

Ride west on Christian Street, away from the Delaware River.

0.15 Hard left on Second Street. Moyamensing Avenue joins Second Street here. Bear left as you turn to stay on Second Street.

0.25 Left on Carpenter Street.

The right side of this alley is lined with eighteenth- and nineteenth-century row homes. The left side was once the location of a smelter that produced lead ammunition. The **Sparks Shot Tower** is still here in the middle of the block. Shot was made by pouring melted lead in droplets from the top of the tower. The drops rounded as they fell, landing in a water tank where they cooled and solidified. This tower, built in 1808 by Thomas Sparks and John Bishop, was the first in the country.

0.35   Left on Front Street at the end of the block.

0.45   Straight across Christian Street.

0.55   Left on Catherine Street.

0.6   Left on **Hancock Street**, an alley between Front and Second Streets.

This is another residential alley with small privately owned eighteenth- and nineteenth-century homes.

0.75   Right on Christian Street.

1.3   Left on Eighth Street.

1.4   Right on Carpenter Street.

1.45   Right on Ninth Street.

The **Italian Market** (M–Sa 9:30–late afternoon, Su 9:30–12:30), dating from the turn of the twentieth century, runs mostly along Ninth Street from Christian Street south to Federal Street and includes more than one hundred merchants. The shops predominantly offer Italian American produce, but there are many others. There are four markets dedicated to cheese and three shops specializing in spices.

A mural of former **Mayor Frank Rizzo,** by Diane Keller with the Mural Arts Program, is on the opposite side of Ninth Street. Rizzo was the Philadelphia police commissioner in the 1960s before he was elected mayor in 1972, and he is still beloved in South Philadelphia.

The Philadelphia Anti-Graffiti Network was established in 1985 by Mayor Wilson Goode primarily to decrease the incidence of graffiti in the city. Artistic murals such as this were more of a side interest at the time. However, two thousand murals later, the legacy of the Anti-Graffiti Network is public art on a grand scale. Now part of the Philadelphia Department of Recreation, the Mural Arts Program paints between seventy and eighty murals each year, and there is a waiting list with hundreds of requests. Most of the murals are created by artists working with local residents and organizations. There is frequently a message the community wants to present, and the artists help develop themes and design images.

Many people have worked on these projects, but Jane Golden deserves much of the credit. She has been the primary talent behind the art and the greatest source of energy propelling this enormous project. Philadelphia's reputation as one the greatest sites of mural art in the country is largely due to Golden's efforts.

1.7 Left on Fitzwater Street.

1.85 Right on Eleventh Street.

2.0 Right on South Street.

The enclosed park on the right is filled with artwork by **Isaiah Zagar**. Zagar began making fantasy mosaics out of tile, pottery, and glass fragments to cope with the aftershock of returning from the Peace Corps in 1968. His work has healed more than his own soul over the years. It has become one of the biggest attractions on South Street and you will see more of it as you ride. Look to the right at the corner of Alder Street to see *Art Is the Center of the World.*

The abstract sculpture of rocks and wire, *Elemental Intervals* by William Freeland, was installed on the façade of a building on the north side of South Street between Tenth and Eleventh Streets.

2.35 Left on Seventh Street.

2.55 Left on Spruce Street.

St. George's Greek Orthodox Cathedral of the Delaware Valley is at 256 South Eighth Street on the left, just north of Spruce Street. John Haviland (Tour 1) designed it in 1822 for St. Andrew's Episcopal Church.

Mikveh Israel Cemetery (Su–Th 10–3 by appointment) is on your right at Darien Street, just before Ninth Street. It is the oldest Jewish

***ART IS THE CENTER OF
THE WORLD* MURAL BY
ISAIAH ZAGAR, TENTH
AND SOUTH STREETS**

cemetery in Philadelphia with possibly as many as five hundred graves. The Mikveh Israel Synagogue was established in 1738, on a Walnut Street site purchased by Nathan Levy from William Penn's son Thomas. There were only a dozen or so Jews in Philadelphia at the time, and no burial grounds were established when Levy's son died the same year. In 1740, Levy, a sea captain who brought the Liberty Bell (Tour 1) to Philadelphia, acquired the land on Darien Street, and the bodies were moved here from Walnut Street. Levy installed a low wall around the graveyard in 1751 to protect the headstones from vandals who used them for target practice.

Nathan Levy is buried here along with many other notable colonial-era Jews, including several veterans of the American Revolution as well as Haym Salomon, who helped finance the war. Rebecca Gratz, who is believed to have been Sir Walter Scott's model for Rebecca in *Ivanhoe*, is buried here as is her brother, Simon, who cofounded the Pennsylvania Academy of Fine Arts.

The Mikveh Israel Congregation now meets on Fourth Street between Market and Arch Streets.

Pennsylvania Hospital (M–F 8:30–5), the first in America, is on the left. The hospital was founded by Ben Franklin and Dr. Thomas Bond (Tour 1) in 1751 to care for the poor, both the physically ill and the insane. Bond and Franklin chose the biblical story of the Good Samaritan as a moral example, and the official seal reads: "Take care of Him and I will repay Thee." Pennsylvania Hospital was the area's leading care facility for mental illness for many years and was also a pioneer in maternal, antenatal, and neonatal care. The oldest surgical theater in the country is located here, first used by the father of American surgery, Dr. Phillip Syng Physick. Today the hospital is part of the health care system of another institution founded by Franklin, the University of Pennsylvania. Caring for the mentally ill is still a specialty of Pennsylvania Hospital, but it is best known for cutting-edge treatments for infertility.

On the next block on your left is **Portico Row**, 900–930 Spruce Street. Thomas Ustick Walter built these sixteen row homes in 1831 and 1832 and sold them to upper-middle-class families. The brick houses were built with marble lintels and Ionic columns supporting a portico that is the entrance to two houses. Sarah Hale, editor of *Godey's Lady's Book*, lived here for several years.

Thomas U. Walter lived from 1804 to 1887 and was a prominent Philadelphia architect. Walter won the competition to design Girard College (Tour 3) and spent fourteen years on that project, which he considered to be his most important work. Walter also designed the

PENNSYLVANIA HOSPITAL, NINTH AND SPRUCE STREETS

expansion wings of the U.S. Capitol Building and the addition of the Capitol dome. He was a consultant on the design of City Hall, taught at the Franklin Institute, and was a founding member of the American Institute of Architecture.

3.05 Left on **Camac Street**.

These houses were originally built in the nineteenth century as homes for people who worked in the mansions on Spruce and Pine Streets. Today they are quiet urban cottages for upscale city residents.

3.15 Left on Pine Street.

Pine Street is lined with nineteenth-century townhouses built for successful professionals and businesspeople.

3.7 Right on Sixth Street.

Mother Bethel African Methodist Episcopal (AME) Church (Tu–Sa 10–3), built in 1889, is on the left at 419 South Sixth Street. The stained glass windows facing Pine Street tell stories from the Bible. Those on Sixth Street represent Jesus. You will see Masonic references on those facing Lombard. These windows were a gift from Prince Hall Masonic Lodge, which was founded at Mother Bethel. The lodge, named for a Boston abolitionist, was the first Masonic temple for African Americans.

The African American Methodist Episcopal Church was founded by Richard Allen. A slave born in 1760, Allen was permanently separated from his family by the time he was seventeen. While in servitude as a field hand in Delaware, Allen was inspired by the sermons of an itinerant preacher who held secret prayer meetings in the woods near the farm. Allen convinced the farm's owner that Christianity would improve the work habits of the slaves, and the owner allowed Reverend Freeborn Garrettson, a Methodist, to preach openly. Garrettson was white and was a former slave-owner, and he now preached not only Christianity but also abolition. He was persuasive enough that Allen's master allowed his slaves to purchase their freedom. In 1780, at the age of twenty, Allen paid $2,000 and left the farm a free man.

Allen continued to practice Methodism because the church was strenuously opposed to slavery, and it also advocated individual responsibility and a strong work ethic. Eventually, he became a preacher in Philadelphia's St. George's Church, the first American Methodist church. Allen's sermons brought many converts to the church, especially among Blacks. White Methodists became anxious about the increasing number of Black congregants and required Blacks to remain in the back of the church. At times, they were not even allowed to sit.

In 1787, a collection was taken and volunteers were employed to expand St. George's by adding an upper gallery. African Americans made major contributions of both time and money. The church elders had determined that the upper gallery was to be for Black members, who would no longer be tolerated in the lower one. Unaware of the plan, Allen and others went to their usual seats for the first service.

During the opening prayer, ushers tried to remove them while they were still on their knees. The strong-arm tactic was the limit of their endurance. After the prayer had finished, Allen and the African-American congregation left as one and did not return.

They joined other Blacks seeking to organize their own religion, but there was much disagreement over which religion was best for the new church. Both the Episcopal Church and the Society of Friends offered support and money; however, Allen still adhered to the tenets of Methodism. The 1793 yellow fever epidemic further delayed the birth of the new church, but it contributed to Allen's fame because he remained in Philadelphia to care for the sick and dying. Legal and financial fights continued between Allen and the Methodist Church until April 9, 1816, when Allen called a conference of the Black Methodist Episcopal Church. The proceedings led to the formation of Mother Bethel African Methodist Episcopal Church, and Allen was elected the first bishop.

Allen continued to fiercely oppose slavery, and he contributed large sums of his own money to assist former slaves. He produced many pamphlets renouncing slavery and advocating assistance to freed slaves. The church was a stop on the Underground Railroad, the dangerous and arduous circuit that helped slaves escape from the South into Canada. He also founded the Free Produce Society, whose members agreed to buy only products of nonslave labor. Allen died on March 26, 1831, and is buried in a tomb beneath Mother Bethel Church.

3.7   Left on Addison Street, the alley between Pine Street and the church.

3.8   Left on Fifth Street.

Look to your right before crossing Spruce Street in one and a half blocks. This section of row houses is called **Girard Row** after Stephen Girard, millionaire banker and financier of the War of 1812 (Tour 3). Girard liked to invest in row houses because he felt he could beautify the city and still make a profit. Girard died before these houses, designed in Greek Revival style by William Struthers, were finished, but his estate completed the project in 1831.

4.0   Right on Locust Street.

From here you can see the **Society Hill Towers** toward the river. Architect I. M. Pei designed them in 1964. By the 1950s, the National Park Service wanted to spruce up Independence Hall and increase tourism, but at that time Society Hill was a slum. In a plan for major urban renewal of the area, in 1958 the Philadelphia Redevelopment Authority held a design competition to construct modern housing here. The winners were Webb and Knapp, for whom Pei worked. Pei also designed a group of three-story townhouses you will see later on this ride.

Society Hill is usually defined as the area from Walnut to Lombard Streets and from Front to Eighth Streets. It takes its name from the Free Society of Traders, a stock company that invested in the original Pennsylvania colony in 1682. The offices were located on Dock Creek, now Dock Street, one of America's first urban blight challenges. The area was an eyesore by the early 1700s, when citizens petitioned the city to clean it up. The creek was filled, derelict buildings were razed, and construction began anew by mid-century. Perhaps the landscape was flattened in the process of filling the creek, but neither the Society nor the Hill lasted past the middle of the eighteenth century.

The area remained moderately prosperous until World War I; however, by mid-twentieth century blight and poverty returned, and it took millions of dollars of federal grants and private investment to renew Society Hill. Construction had continued during the intervening two hundred years, and it was necessary to demolish existing buildings if new ones were to be built. The planners made as many heroic efforts as possible to save the buildings erected before the mid-1800s, but most buildings constructed after that time were destroyed. Many urban renewal projects have failed in this country, but thanks to a very large coordinated effort and to the intrinsic value of so many of the colonial buildings, Society Hill today is one of Philadelphia's most prosperous neighborhoods.

4.1   Straight across Fourth Street into **Bingham Court**.

I. M. Pei designed the row homes of Bingham Court in 1967, five years after he designed the Society Hill Towers. Planners wanted thoroughly modern housing to attract residents and to create living neighborhoods existing elbow to elbow with historic colonial homes. Although the towers made a dramatic difference to the skyline, adding ultramodern concrete and glass high-rises amid the low surrounding buildings, the townhouses in contrast were built to blend in with the eighteenth-century homes around them. To achieve this, Pei used red brick in a Flemish bond pattern that was popular in the 1700s. He also kept the houses low and arranged them around a brick courtyard. The sculpture in the courtyard, installed here in 1969, is *Unity* by Richard Lieberman.

4.12   Left in Bingham Court to Willings Alley.

4.15   Left on Willings Alley.

This tiny alley hides the first legal Catholic church in the English-speaking world. On the north side of the alley a gated arch leads to a courtyard. There you will find **Old St. Joseph's Church** (daily 11–4), built in 1838. It is the third building on this site.

Jesuit Father Joseph Greaton came to Philadelphia in 1729. At that time, it was illegal to hold a Catholic mass outside of private homes in the British Empire. Greaton built a chapel inside his house in 1733, and the next year he successfully tested in court William Penn's Charter of Privileges, which declared freedom of religion for all. The first Catholic church was then erected here in 1755.

The courtyard and unobtrusive entrance were purposely so designed because anti-Catholic sentiment was strong and occasionally violent. In 1844, other Catholic churches in Philadelphia were burned to the ground by rioting mobs. The almost-hidden nature of St. Joseph's was considered to be its salvation.

4.2   Left on Fourth Street.

The **Philadelphia Contributionship for Insuring Houses from Loss by**

Fire is on the opposite side of Fourth Street, at number 212. It was designed in 1835 by Thomas U. Walter. The mansard roof was added in 1866. This is the first permanent home of the insurance company, founded by Ben Franklin in 1752. The company met in taverns and coffeehouses before this building was completed. The design is Greek Revival and is adapted from Walter's Portico Row at Ninth and Spruce Streets.

The **Shippen-Wistar house**, built in 1765, is on your right on the next block at 238 South Fourth Street. Dr. William Shippen, a prominent Philadelphia physician, built this home for his son. The house was later bought by Dr. Caspar Wistar, another well-known eighteenth-century physician. Wistar was an avid horticulturist, and the purple-flowering vine wisteria is named after him.

The **Cadwalader house** is to the left, adjacent to the Shippen-Wister house at 240 South Fourth Street. It was the headquarters of the Mutual Assurance Company (also known as the Green Tree) from 1836 to 1987. This was the second fire insurance company in America and, unlike Franklin's company, they insured houses with trees in front. The offices of the Episcopal Church now occupy both the Shippen-Wistar and the Cadwalader houses.

Old St. Mary's Church is immediately after the Cadwalader House, and also on your right at 252 South Fourth Street between Locust and Spruce. St. Mary's was founded in 1763, and the building has been modified many times. It was the second Catholic church and the first cathedral in Philadelphia and was burned in the anti-Catholic riots of 1844.

The magnificent Federal-style house on the left just after the corner of Cypress and Fourth Streets at number 321 is the **Hill-Physick-Keith House** (June–Aug., Th–Sa 12–4; Sept.–May, Th–Sa 12–2), the only remaining freestanding eighteenth-century mansion in Old City. In 1786, when it was built, there were many mansions interspersed between rows of smaller homes. There are a total of thirty-two rooms in the house, including a ballroom on the first floor. The fan light over the front door is especially beautiful. The first owner was Colonel Henry Hill, a wealthy wine merchant who died of yellow fever in 1793.

Dr. Phillip Syng Physick, father of American surgery, owned the house from 1815 to 1837. Physick practiced at Pennsylvania Hospital, where he was the first surgeon to use catgut sutures and where he invented the stomach pump.

4.4   Left on Pine Street.

Old Pine Presbyterian Church (M–F 10–3) is on the right at 412 Pine Street. In spite of the fact that Presbyterians constituted the largest religious group in the colonies, this is the only prerevolutionary Presbyterian church still standing in America. It was built by colonial-era master carpenter Robert Smith (Tour 1) in 1768, and John Frazer made major changes to the façade in 1837 and 1857. Inventor and astronomer David Rittenhouse (Tour 4) is buried in the graveyard, as is Eugene Ormandy, beloved principal conductor of the Philadelphia Orchestra from 1938 to 1980. The orchestra became renowned for its unusual, lush sound, a result of Ormandy's emphasis on stringed instruments.

4.45   Left onto St. Peter's Way.

Walk your bike through this parklike corridor. Cross Delancey Street, which is a delightful surprise in the middle of the city. It is a tiny row of homes, walkways, and parks. These so-called greenways were part of the total plan for Society Hill as envisioned by Edmund Bacon in the 1950s. Bacon recognized the importance of semi-isolated areas with public parks, gardens, and small homes to keep the neighborhoods comfortable for family living.

Walk straight through **Three Bears Park,** named for *Family of Bears,* a concrete sculpture by Sherl Joseph Winter installed here in 1966.

4.5   Left on Cypress Street.

4.55   Cross Fourth Street.

There is an intriguing house on the right about halfway up the block with interesting terra-cotta sculpture along the stairs leading to the house.

Be sure to take a look at *Kangaroos* created in 1970 by Harold Kimmelman, located at the end of the street on the right.

4.6   Left on Lawrence Court.

4.7   Left on Pine Street.

St. Peter's Church (daily 9–5), on the right between Third and Fourth Streets, was built by Robert Smith from 1758 to 1761. St. Peter's Church was erected when Christ Church in Old City became too small for its growing congregation. Thomas Penn donated the land; he eschewed his father's Quaker beliefs and joined the Anglican Church. Dr. John Kearsley, who directed Christ Church, supervised the construction of the new church. This church is more subdued than Christ Church, and its large Palladian window is not as ornate as the one on its northern sister. The original pews are still in place. William Strickland, one of Philadelphia's most prominent architects, added the steeple in 1852.

Among those buried here are Dr. John Morgan, founder of the first American medical school, prominent colonial merchants Benjamin Chew and Nicholas Biddle, and artist Charles Willson Peale.

The **Kosciuszko National Memorial** (June–Oct., daily 9–5; Nov.–May, W–Su 9–5) is on the left at Third Street. Joseph Few, a member of the Carpenters' Company, built this Georgian house in 1775.

Tadeusz (Thaddeus) Kosciuszko (1746–1817) was a Polish army officer who served in two revolutions, first in America and then in Poland. He was born into a wealthy family and received an excellent education that included military training. He became a tutor and fell in love with one of his students, the daughter of a prominent Polish general, and attempted unsuccessfully to elope with her. In 1776 Kosciuszko fled her father's wrath by emigrating to the American colonies, where he joined the Continental Army as a civil engineer.

Kosciuszko is credited with planning military fortifications, orchestrating blockades and rescuing the army by directing two dangerous river crossings. By the end of the war, he received U.S. citizenship and a promotion to brigadier general.

Kosciuszko returned to Poland in 1784 and assumed control of his family's estate. One of his first acts was to free the family's serfs, a noble deed that reduced him to poverty for several years.

Poland faced decades of political turmoil, and Kosciuszko remained steadfastly devoted to the rights of the common people. When revolution broke out, he was chosen to command the Polish Army. To increase the forces, Kosciuszko granted freedom to serfs who volunteered. Although unpopular with Polish nobility, it did produce a huge army of peasants wielding pikes and scythes. The uprising ultimately failed, however, and Kosciuszko was wounded and taken prisoner. When he was released in 1797 he returned to Philadelphia and received a hero's welcome. In time, he freed his American slaves and sold part of his estate to pay for their education and transition to freedom.

When Kosciuszko died in 1817, his body was returned to Poland and buried in 1819 among the tombs of kings in Krakow's cathedral. The citizens revived an age-old custom of building giant earthen mounds to commemorate their heroes, and they erected a monument to Kosciuszko outside the city.

4.9   Right on Second Street.

You'll get a nice view of the **Head House** and **Market Shed** as you near Lombard Street. The first markets in the city were open sheds in the center of High Street, now Market Street. Joseph Wharton, a merchant, and Mayor Edward Shippen built this market shed in 1745. The current head house was built in 1804 and is the oldest in America. It was used to store fire equipment and as a meeting place for volunteer firefighters.

5.05   Cross South Street.

The song "South Street" was a hit in the 1950s. The street has certainly changed since then, but it is still one of the most active night spots in Philadelphia. There are numerous shops and boutiques and many restaurants.

5.25   Left on Fitzwater Street.

You will twist and turn here a bit to see the mix of old and new townhouses along these little streets.

5.3   Left on Front Street.

5.4   Left on Kenilworth Street.

5.5   Left on Second Street.

5.7   Left on Queen Street.

An old stable on the left was converted into townhouses. Look for the statue of a fireman running to a fire with his dog at his side. This was commissioned as part of a Philadelphia Redevelopment Authority ordinance that requires developers to provide public art worth 1 percent of their total development costs.

5.9   Right on Swanson Street.

5.95 Right on Christian Street.

6.0   End at Gloria Dei Church.

ATTRACTIONS IN SOUTH PHILADELPHIA

Gloria Dei, or Old Swedes', Church, 916 South Swanson Street (215) 389-1513, daily 9–5, http://www.nps.gov/glde, free.

Hill-Physick-Keith House, 321 South Fourth Street (215) 925-7866, June–Aug., Th–Sa 12–4; Sept.–May, Th–Sa 12–2, admission.

Italian Market, Ninth Street between Christian and Federal Streets, M–Sa 9:30–late afternoon, Su 9:30–12:30, http://www.italianmarket.com, free.

Mikveh Israel Cemetery, Spruce Street, between Eighth and Ninth Streets (215) 922-5446, Su–Th 10–3, by appointment, free.

Mother Bethel African Methodist Episcopal Church, 419 South Sixth Street (215) 925-0616, Tu–Sa 10–3, free.

Old Pine Presbyterian Church, 412 Pine Street (215) 925-8051, M–F 10–3, free.

Old St. Joseph's Catholic Church, 321 Willings Alley (215) 923-1733, daily 11–4, http://www.oldstjoseph.org, free.

Old St. Mary's Catholic Church, 252 South Fourth Street (215) 923-7930, daily 9–5, free.

Pennsylvania Hospital, 800 Spruce Street (215) 829-3461, M–F 8:30–5, call for guided tours, free.

St. Peter's Church, Third and Pine Streets (215) 925-5968, daily 9–5, free.

Thaddeus Kosciuszko National Memorial, 301 Pine Street (215) 597-9618, June–Oct., daily 9–5; Nov.–May, W–Su 9–5.

City Hall and the Parkway

DISTANCE: 7.3 miles, 12 km

TERRAIN: Flat. Paved roads in city traffic. You should walk your bike about two blocks around City Hall.

START: Gallery Shopping Mall at Ninth and Market Streets.

ACCESS BY CAR: From **I-676,** take the Eighth Street exit for Independence Hall. Go south on Eighth Street for three blocks to Market Street. Right on Market Street. There is a parking garage on Ninth Street between Market and Arch Streets.

ACCESS BY PUBLIC TRANSPORTATION: All **SEPTA Regional Rail Lines** stop at the Market East Station. Ride one block south on Tenth Street. Turn left on Market Streets and ride east one block. The **Market/Frankford High Speed Line** stops at Eighth and Market. Ride one block west to Ninth Street. The **Broad Street High Speed Line** stops at Broad and Market Streets (City Hall). Ride six blocks east on Market Street.

SERVICES: The Gallery (at the start), the Reading Terminal Market (mile 0.3), and Liberty Place (mile 5.6) have a variety of food offerings as well as public restrooms. The Free Library (mile 1.2) and City Hall (mile 6.1) also have public restrooms.

BIKE SHOPS: Bike Line, 1028 Arch Street (215) 923-1310 (mile 0.15) and **Cycle Sport,** 2329 Brown Street (215) 765-9100 (not on the route).

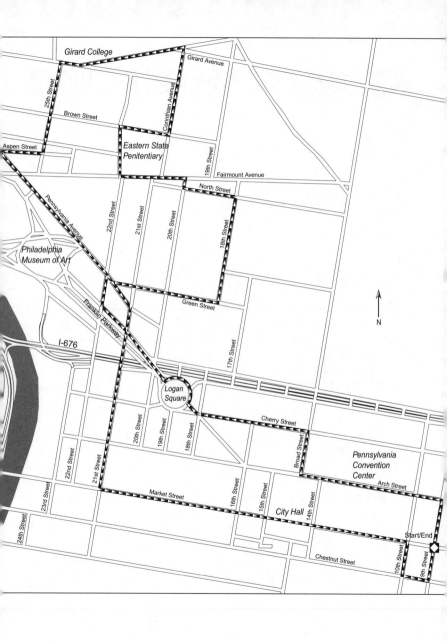

The Benjamin Franklin Parkway extends diagonally across northwest Center City and was designed to be America's Champs-Elysées. The view is unobstructed from City Hall to the Philadelphia Museum of Art and is enhanced by the fountains and sculptures at Logan Square and Eakins Oval. Several buildings, including the Free Library and the Franklin Institute, were designed along with the Parkway to give it a unified and monumental appearance.

The first anchor of the Parkway is City Hall, a building that was obsolete before it was completed and was almost demolished only a few decades later. Fortunately, the beautiful Beaux-Arts masonry structure is still with us.

This ride begins a bit east of City Hall before taking you along the parkway. You will meander through the art museum district, a quiet and increasingly affluent neighborhood, and ride on to Eastern State Penitentiary and Girard College. You will complete your circuit with a tour of the new commercial district along Market Street and then of City Hall's courtyard.

0.0 Start by riding north on Ninth Street from Market Street past the **Gallery** (M, Tu, Th, Sa 10–7, W, F 10–8, Su 12–5), an indoor shopping mall.

0.14 Left on Arch Street.

The boundaries of Philadelphia's **Chinatown** are approximately from Eighth and Arch Streets to Twelfth and Vine Streets. The area's ethnic identity began during the Civil War with a Chinese laundry at 913 Race Street. Within ten years, the same building housed the city's first Chinese restaurant. The longest continually operating restaurant in the area is the Magic Fan, which opened in 1948. Chinatown experienced an economic boom in the 1990s, when the number of restaurants and shops more than tripled. The cuisine also changed from mostly Americanized fare to more authentic dishes from several regions in China as well as Thailand and Vietnam. A strong Asian-American community here is committed to maintaining a safe and prosperous neighborhood. Residents successfully fought a proposal to construct a new sports stadium here in the 1990s, because it would disrupt residential sections of Chinatown.

China Gate on your right on Tenth Street was designed by local architect Sabrina Soong and was funded by a grant from the National Endowment for the Arts. The design is based on the style of the Qing Dynasty, which ruled from the seventeenth to the early twentieth centuries. Philadelphia's sister city in China, Tianjinn, provided the tiles as well as a team of engineers and artisans to construct the arch in 1984.

The **Reading Terminal Market** (M–Sa 8–6), on the left at Twelfth Street, is considered one of the best farmers' markets in the country There are more than eighty merchants selling fresh produce, baked goods, handmade crafts, and prepared foods, most locally produced. The building was constructed in 1889 by the Reading Railroad as a train shed. While trains ran on the upper floor, a grand food market opened on the lower floor in 1892, with 7,800 square feet of vendor stalls. This was during the heyday of train service, and Reading sought to lure passengers with not only a dizzying array of vendors but also personalized services. Passengers could place an order for groceries, which was filled by vendors and loaded on the train to be picked up when the passengers reached their stop. The market dwindled to sixty-four vendors during the 1930s but was thriving again during World War II. By the 1970s, however, the railroad was failing, and the market slipped into decline for several years. The presence of the Gallery and other new businesses generated new interest in the market, and it thrived again in the 1980s. The decision to construct the convention center across the street secured the comeback, and today there are some eight thousand visitors each week.

The **Pennsylvania Convention Center** is on the right between Eleventh and Thirteenth Streets. The old train shed of the Reading Railroad was converted into the grand hall of the convention center. The two buildings that make up the convention center encompass four city blocks and were built between 1993 and 1994.

PENNSYLVANIA ACADEMY OF THE FINE ARTS, BROAD AND CHERRY STREETS

0.45 Right on Broad Street.

0.65 Left on Cherry Street.

The **Pennsylvania Academy of the Fine Arts** (Tu–Sa 10-5, Su 11–5) is on the corner of Broad and Cherry Streets. In 1805, two of America's earliest master artists, painter Charles Willson Peale and sculptor William Rush, helped found the academy. It was located in Independence Hall until the current building opened in 1876. This building is one of the most famous Frank Furness designs (Tour 7).

The human form itself was a source of scandal for the academy for a century. The first attempt to create a school for fine arts failed because of disagreement over the use of live models. And an early academy exhibit at Independence Hall that included plasters of nudes created heated debate until the establishment of special Ladies' Day events, when "offensive" statues were decorously draped. Later, painter Thomas Eakins was forced to resign his position with the academy when he removed the loincloth from a male model in front of female students. Ironically, one of the academy's greatest strengths has always been its anatomy program. Students heard lectures from physicians, and Eakins held classes in human and animal dissection.

The academy continues to train fine artists in painting, sculpture, and printmaking. In addition to its own four-year programs, it offers B.F.A. and M.F.A. degrees in cooperation with the University of Pennsylvania (Tour 10) and the University of the Arts (Tour 4). The permanent exhibition includes a comprehensive survey of eighteenth- to twentieth-century painting and sculpture.

The **Friends Meeting Center** is on the northwest corner of Fifteenth and Cherry Streets. Commonly called Quakers, the Society of Friends has its roots in seventeenth-century England, where Quakers, like Puritans, were persecuted. It is estimated that as many as fifteen thousand Quakers were jailed under the Quaker Act of 1662. Philadelphia's founder, William Penn, was a Quaker, and his influence assured that Friends were not mistreated in Pennsylvania. In fact, Quaker beliefs dominated the colony's earliest laws. In other American colonies, however, Quakers often suffered the same persecution they sought to escape in England. The statue in front of the meeting house is **Mary Dyer,** who was a seventeenth-century Quaker hanged in Massachusetts for her religious beliefs. The artist is Sylvia Shaw Judson, who is also a Quaker.

The **United Fund Headquarters,** now the United Way, is on the right between Seventeenth and Eighteenth Streets. Long-term plans for the Parkway restrict the design and size of buildings that abut it. Designed by the prestigious Philadelphia architecture firm Mitchell/Giurgola Associates, this small, modern building built in 1969 conforms to the unusual shape of the site. Each face of the building is unique to accommodate differences in sunlight exposure. The north face is almost all glass to let in as much light as possible, the west wall has solid sunscreens to shade that façade, and the south side has recessed windows to limit the heat and light but allow unimpeded views.

0.95 Bear right onto the **Benjamin Franklin Parkway**.

Calls for a roadway to run diagonally from City Hall to Fairmount Park arose in the late nineteenth century, but actual work did not begin until 1907, with plans by Paul Philippe Cret, Horace Trumbauer, Jacques Greber, and C. Clark Zantzinger. Eli Price Kirk was the guiding hand of the project, supplying the drive and ambition needed to see the long process through to completion. Cret and Greber worked out the details of Kirk's desire for an American Champs-Elysées that would link the center of the city with Fairmount Park. Plans were already in place for City Hall, and Kirk wanted something equally monumental to anchor the opposite end of the parkway. He was enthusiastic when a new art museum was proposed and Trumbauer was chosen to design it.

The **Bell Atlantic Tower,** constructed in 1991, is on the left at Seventeenth Street. This is my favorite of the buildings that rose in the last decades of the twentieth century. Prior to that time, there was a gentlemen's agreement not to build anything higher than the top of William Penn's hat on City Hall.

1.0 Pull over onto the sidewalk at the intersection with Eighteenth Street, and look around before continuing.

A statue of **Thaddeus Kosciuszko** by Marian Konieczny is on the left at Eighteenth and Race Streets. This was a gift from the Polish people in 1976. Kosciuszko was a hero of both the American and the Polish revolutions. His story of personal sacrifice to oppressed people is told in Tour 2.

The official name of the circle within a square at this intersection is **Logan Square,** although you will hear it called Logan Circle by those who drive around it. As one of William Penn's original five open squares, it was formerly called Northwest Square and was used as a graveyard and for public executions until 1823. It was named for Penn's secretary James Logan in 1825.

The **Swann Memorial Fountain** by Alexander Stirling Calder dominates Logan Square. The design is in homage to Dr. Wilson Cary

Swann, who was active in the effort to bring clean water to city residents through public fountains. An Indian man and a leaping fish symbolize the Delaware River, and two Indian women portray the Schuylkill River and Wissahickon Creek. Both women are holding Swanns, that is, swans.

The **Cathedral of Saints Peter and Paul** is on the corner of Eighteenth Street. This still-active church is the oldest building on Logan Square and predates the earliest Parkway plans. It was built in Italian Renaissance style from 1846 to 1864.

There are several sculptures placed around the fountain in Logan Square. Near the sidewalk close to the cathedral is the statue *Jesus Breaking Bread* by Walter Erlebacher, dating to 1978. On the right at Eighteenth Street and the parkway is **Kopernik,** by Dudley Talcott, created in 1973. Nikolaj Kopernik was better known as Nicolaus Copernicus, the Polish astronomer famed for postulating that the earth revolves around the sun. Along Eighteenth Street, between Race and Vine Streets, are statues of **Thomas FitzSimons** (Giuseppe Donato, 1946), who signed the U.S. Constitution, and **Diego de Gardoqui,** an eighteenth-century envoy of the king of Spain. As you continue along the Parkway toward the art museum, you will pass the **General Galusha Pennypacker Memorial,** by Albert Laessle, dating to 1934. At age twenty-two, Pennypacker was the youngest general in the U.S. Army during the Civil War. This work is a good example of the exuberant and highly detailed Beaux-Arts style.

Behind General Pennypacker, look at the **Family Court Building**. This building was part of the original Parkway design along with the Free Library, both of which were based on the Place de la Concorde in Paris.

After passing the fountain but before crossing Twentieth Street, you will come to the **Shakespeare Memorial** on the right. On top of a black marble pedestal, Hamlet sits contemplating life's tragedies while the jester Touchstone tilts his head back in laughter. Installed in 1928, this work is also by Alexander Stirling Calder and is considered by many to be Calder's best work.

Behind the Shakespeare memorial is the Greek Revival–style **Free**

Library of Philadelphia (M–Th 9–9, F 9–6, Sa 9–5). Horace Trumbauer worked on the library between 1917 and 1927. Ben Franklin created this country's first library in 1731; however, when the American Library Association was founded in Philadelphia in 1876, there were no free, public libraries here, although such libraries did exist in other American cities. Dr. William Pepper, a provost for the University of Pennsylvania, waged an energetic campaign to form a free library in the late 1800s. He convinced his wealthy uncle George Pepper to bequeath $250,000 to the city, and the Philadelphia Free Library was founded in 1894. When William Pepper died four years later, the library was the largest in the world with 250,000 books and a circulation of 1.7 million. A referendum for a new building was passed in 1897, but construction was delayed until 1917; this building opened ten years later. This is now the Central Library and there are fifty-five branches throughout the city. It remains one of the greatest of America's libraries. The Rare Books Department is especially notable, with five-thousand-year-old cuneiform tablets and a vast collection of European and Oriental manuscripts from the ninth to the eighteenth centuries. The library hosts numerous events free to the public, including lectures, exhibitions, and readings, and it remains a valuable asset to the city.

The **Franklin Institute** (Science Center daily 9:30–5, Mandell Center Su–Th 9:30–5, F–Sa 9:30–9) is on the left at Twentieth Street. Built from 1932 to 1934 by John T. Windrim, this is Philadelphia's science and technology museum, visited by twice as many people annually as the Philadelphia Museum of Art. It was founded in 1824 and was originally located at 15 South Seventh Street, where the Atwater Kent Museum is today. In 1990, the Mandell Futures Center was built across Twentieth Street, placed so that it is not seen from the Parkway. This modern-style building has numerous interactive exhibits, updated frequently, exploring scientific advances.

The **All Wars Memorial to Colored Soldiers and Sailors** is in front of the Franklin Institute. Until the 1990s this memorial, created by J. Otto Schweizer in 1934, was located on an infrequently used road behind Memorial Hall in West Fairmount Park. A vigorous public campaign succeeded in relocating it to this more prominent position. The **Civil War Soldiers and Sailors Memorial** is on both sides of the Parkway at Twentieth Street. It was designed by Hermon Atkins MacNeil in 1927.

The **Rodin Museum** (Tu–Su 10–5) is on the right between Twenty-first and Twenty-second Streets. The architects were Paul Philippe Cret and Jacques Greber, the principal designers of the Parkway. The museum is in the form of a classical temple and is behind castings of Rodin's most famous works, *The Thinker* and *The Gates of Hell.*

THE THINKER BY AUGUSTE RODIN, TWENTY-FIRST STREET AND THE BENJAMIN FRANKLIN PARKWAY

1.5   Right on Twenty-second Street.

The **Parkway House** is on Twenty-second Street at Pennsylvania Avenue on the right. This International-style building was built in 1952 and is one of the first post–World War II luxury apartment buildings in the city.

1.6   Left on Pennsylvania Avenue.

1.85   Right on Twenty-fourth Street.

1.9   Quick right on Green Street.

St. Francis Xavier Catholic Church is on the left on Green Street. Lining both sides of the street are **Victorian mansions** built between 1860 and 1890. The brownstones at **2144** and **2146** are attributed to the Victorian-era architect Wilson Eyre (Tour 4).

You have now entered the Fairmount neighborhood. Named for the hill on which the Philadelphia Museum of Art stands, Fairmount is just north of the museum. A mix of row homes, apartment buildings, corner stores, and restaurants, it is a neighborhood built by immigrants and has become gentrified in the past decade.

2.45   Left on Eighteenth Street.

2.55   Left on North Street.

2.7   Right on Twentieth Street.

2.75   Left on Fairmount Avenue.

The massive granite medieval fortress on the right at Twenty-first Street is **Eastern State Penitentiary** (April 16–Nov. 30, W–Su 10–5, optional guided tours on the hour, half hour Sa and Su P.M., last tour at 4), designed by John Haviland and built between 1822 and 1836. By 1776, Philadelphia's first jail, Old Stone Jail, was overcrowded, filthy, and disease ridden. A second jail, built on Walnut Street, was not much better but was used through the Revolutionary War. By 1787, concerned citizens led by Dr. Benjamin Rush founded the Philadelphia

Society for Alleviating the Miseries of Public Prisons, now known as the Pennsylvania Prison Society.

Rush and his followers lobbied for construction of a new prison to house 250 inmates. Funds were appropriated in 1790, and a competition was held for the design. The rules stated that the building should feel imposing, striking fear into the hearts of potential residents. Haviland's design won, but only after years of delays and disagreements did construction finally begin in 1822. The prison opened in 1829, nearly forty years after the project was approved.

The interior was originally designed as seven radial arms around a central hub. Cells line both sides of the arms and the hub was the center of observation and operation. This design was copied around the world in more than three hundred prisons, including ones in London, Paris, Berlin, Madrid, Milan, Copenhagen, Dublin, and Beijing. The eight-by-twelve-foot cells, lit with skylights, were designed to house a single convict, who was provided with a bed, a stool, a small table, and a Bible. Each cell opened into a courtyard for exercise, but the courtyards were also separated from each other to prevent contact between inmates. Prisoners were allowed only rare visits from friends and family, and cells had feeding slots to minimize contact with guards. Soon after the prison opened, the inmates' program of solitary reflection was augmented with work in shoemaking, weaving, or other jobs.

This so-called Pennsylvania system of solitary confinement was supposed to facilitate quiet contemplation of the Bible, leading the prisoner to become penitent, hence the new term to describe it: penitentiary. It was loosely based on the Quaker belief that every person has an inner light that can be reached by introspection, and the common view that cloistered monks and nuns received divine inspiration from their solitude. Although voluntary solitude may have had the desired effect, forced isolation induced insanity. Today, solitary confinement is used sparingly as a harsh punishment and not for rehabilitation. However, the Pennsylvania system became obsolete in 1913 for a different reason: the number of inmates increased so dramatically that the system of putting one prisoner per cell became an inefficient use of space and was discontinued.

Cell blocks were added to meet the increasing population until 1926, when there was no room left between the radial arms. The first three arms were a single story, but the later cell blocks were two and then three stories tall. Fourteen cell blocks eventually housed 1,700 inmates rather than the original 250. Al Capone was incarcerated here for eight months in 1929 and 1930. Capone furnished his cell with antiques and original artwork, and routinely had parties with the guards.

The penitentiary closed in 1970 and over the next twenty-four years, the fate of the building was in jeopardy. It was used for storage but was severely vandalized. A forest of weeds grew from the ground through the second and third stories, breaking up the cement and stone blocks. There were plans to demolish it and plans to sell it for commercial use. Finally, Eastern State Task Force, a group of architects, historians and preservationists, persuaded the city to save the building. Through the efforts of many foundations, Eastern State Penitentiary opened for public tours in 1994, receiving more than ten thousand visitors that first year. It remains a popular tourist attraction, especially on Bastille Day and during the month before Halloween, when there are special tours to commemorate those events.

2.95 Right on Twenty-second Street.

3.1 Right on Brown Street.

3.25 Left on Corinthian Avenue.

3.5 Left on Girard Avenue.

The Greek temple in front of you is **Founder's Hall of Girard College**. Just past the college gates, you can see a statue of Stephen Girard surrounded by children.

Born and raised in France, Girard went to sea in 1764 at the age of fourteen, perhaps to escape the chaos of his extended family, which included twenty children. By 1774, he commanded his own ship and traded in the West Indies and the American colonies. British blockade of American ports during the Revolution forced Girard ashore for the duration, and he settled in Philadelphia. Following the war he resumed his sea trade, amassing many ships and a great fortune to become Philadelphia's wealthiest citizen and a major financier of the War of 1812.

Girard was known for his humanitarian actions, including his personal care of victims of the yellow fever epidemic of 1793. During that horrific summer, 10 percent of Philadelphia's population died and more than half moved away. Girard stayed in the city to tend to the ill and dying and to help bury the dead.

When Girard died in 1833, he left most of his fortune to charitable institutions and bequeathed $2 million to establish Girard College on a forty-five-acre site. The college was to provide a home and an education for white, fatherless boys. The college became the focus of a long, fierce civil rights struggle that succeeded with the admission of nonwhites in 1968. Girls were not admitted until 1984.

Founder's Hall of Girard College, built from 1833 to 1847, was designed by Thomas Ustick Walter in Greek Revival style. Walter's designs were in accordance with the wish of Girard College board director Nicholas Biddle, who wanted the building to be the most perfect reconstruction of a Greek temple in America. Girard's tomb is on the first floor.

3.8   Left on Ringgold Street, immediately after Twenty-fourth Street.

Turn immediately after the **St. Nicholas Ukrainian Catholic Church** on the left. It is highly visible with its gold onion dome and iconic mosaic of Jesus.

4.05   Right on Aspen Street at the "T."

4.25   Left on Twenty-seventh Street and immediately left again on Pennsylvania Avenue.

The **Fidelity Mutual Life Insurance Company Building**, one of the best examples of Art Deco style in Philadelphia, is on the left at the corner of Twenty-sixth Street and Pennsylvania Avenue. It was constructed in 1925 as part of the Benjamin Franklin Parkway project but in a more modern style than many of the other Parkway buildings. The building is now owned by the Philadelphia Museum of Art.

4.85 Bear left on Hamilton Street.

4.9 Right on Twenty-first Street.

You will ride under the train tracks and John F. Kennedy Boulevard. The boulevard runs from the Schuylkill River to Broad Street and was built in the 1950s. Before then, dozens of railroad tracks ran along what was called the Chinese Wall, which separated this area from Center City.

5.55 Left on Market Street.

Market Street, usually quite busy, is lined with several large and imposing office buildings. Here you will pass some of Philadelphia's most famous (but not necessarily aesthetically pleasing) art. We are now heading back to City Hall.

Commerce Square is between Twentieth and Twenty-first Streets. But you can see the keyhole tops from far and wide. Look at these buildings from the Schuylkill Expressway when they are silhouetted by the sun, and you will see why they are known as Mickey and Minnie. These buildings were designed by Pei Cobb Freed and Partners in 1987. Pei also designed the Society Hill Towers and Bingham Court (Tour 2).

The tops of the **Mellon Bank Center** and **One** and **Two Liberty Place,** located between Sixteenth and Eighteenth Streets, are visible from all over the city. The Mellon Bank Center is the steel and glass structure crowned with the combination pyramid and pagoda on the left at Eighteenth Street; it was built in 1990. The Liberty Place buildings, to the right after Seventeenth Street, are the glass and steel skyscrapers with the chevron tops, also built in 1990.

For better or worse, these were the first buildings to rise above William Penn's hat. Before 1990, there had been a standing gentlemen's agreement to keep Billy's bonnet the highest fixture in the city, reminiscent of medieval discussions about the height of palaces versus the height of church spires. As a Quaker, Penn would undoubtedly be dismayed by such attention to his image.

The **Penn Center Complex** is on the left between Eighteenth and Fifteenth Streets. Its various parts were constructed between 1953 and 1982, after the Chinese Wall came down and before the chevrons and "mouse ears" went up. The best view on Market Street is the fabulous black and gold façade of **Suburban Station,** on the left at Sixteenth Street, built between 1924 and 1929.

6.05 Dismount your bike and cross Fifteenth Street in the crosswalk toward. Walk across Center Square toward **City Hall** (M–F 9:30–4:15, self-guided tower tours, one-hour interior tour daily at 12:30).

This was William Penn's Center Square, chosen to be the location of municipal buildings. Most of the city's population, however, lived along the Delaware River until well into the nineteenth century, and City Hall remained at Independence Hall until Mayor Edwin Henry Fitler moved his office here in 1889. Although architect John MacArthur presented his plans in 1871, the building was not finished until 1901, and at that time the rest of the city offices moved here. Seven more mayors served in the incomplete structure. It was to be the tallest building in the world, but by 1901 both the Eiffel Tower and the Washington Monument were taller. At 547 feet, however, it is still the tallest masonry-supported building in the world. During its construction, the science of steel framing advanced, and masonry construction for large buildings became obsolete. The style is Second Empire, the same as the Louvre in Paris; it is one of the styles associated with the Beaux-Arts movement.

Almost all of the sculptures are the work of Alexander Milne Calder, father of the artist who created the Swann Memorial Fountain and the Shakespeare Memorial, both of which you have seen on this tour. The third-generation Calder is the modernist sculptor Alexander Calder; he uses no middle name and is frequently called Sandy.

Alexander Milne Calder was born in Scotland. He was trained as a stonecutter and studied in Paris and London. In 1868, at the age of

had important and influential members of society among
People have always longed to hobnob with the rich and
after the looting and pillaging dropped off, the masons
onmasons were petitioning to join up. All the secrecy
allure. As working masons were replaced with high soci-
, they started using the term "speculative masons" to
society.

miss the *Clothespin* on the west side of Center Square.
bly Philadelphia's most famous work of public art, much
n of many. It was created by Claes Oldenburg in 1976.
lights in making monumental pieces out of common util-
He was inspired to do this piece while flying over a city
hat the buildings looked the same size as a clothespin he
He also made the giant *Split Button* for the University of
(Tour 10).

ated by Robert Engman in 1975, is on the south side of
ngman taught graduate studies in sculpture at the Univer-
lvania before he was appointed to the City Art Commis-
k Rizzo's predecessor. Rizzo promptly fired him, and
rned to the university, where he created *Triune*. The work
ioned by Girard and Fidelity Banks as part of their obli-
City Council ordinance that requires developers to donate
public art 1 percent of the total cost of their building proj-

cKinley (Charles Albert Lopez and Isidore Konti, 1908)
south side of City Hall. President McKinley was assassi-
l, and three days later, the *Philadelphia Inquirer* began a
iption series to commission a memorial. Lopez was cho-
soon after finishing the models, and Konti completed the

Center Square by riding east on Market Street.

Art Deco building on the left is **One East Penn Square**.
e-skyscraper was built in 1930 by Ritter and Shay, who
st impact on Philadelphia's skyline during the 1920s and

twenty-two, he sailed to New York but soon realized there was more
opportunity for a sculptor in the rapidly expanding city of Philadelphia. In 1873, at the age of twenty-seven, he was selected by John
MacArthur to sculpt what would ultimately be more than 250 works
for City Hall. At twenty-six tons and thirty-seven feet tall, **Billy Penn**
was perched atop the building in 1894 after two years of discussions
about how to get it up there. Much to Calder's horror, it was mounted
facing northeast. Calder claims that he intended Penn to face south,
facing the track of the sun, and he believed the change to be a deliber-
ate personal affront. Officials insisted that it was always intended to
face northeast toward Penn Treaty Park, the location of Penn's negoti-
ations with the Lenape Indians.

The other statues are allegorical and historical works. At the top of
the roof are twenty-five-foot figures representing the four populated
continents: **Asia, America, Europe,** and **Africa.** Within the dormers,
below the pediments, are animals and humans representing each continent. Below the dormers are seven stories that appear as three tiers.
The statues in the upper tier represent human virtues. The figures in the
middle tier show the pursuits of knowledge such as history, art, and science. The bottom tier has human forms that signify American workers.
And in the keystones above the four archways are the faces of **William
Penn, Ben Franklin, Moses,** and **Sympathy.**

City Hall has had an embattled history. Early detractors called it the
"tower of folly" and the "marble elephant." By the 1950s it was considered hopelessly out of fashion and ugly. The enormous cost was the
only reason it wasn't demolished and replaced with the same kinds of
buildings that now line JFK Boulevard.

North of City Hall toward Arch Street is a statue of **General George
McClellan** (Henry Jackson, 1894) astride his horse. McClellan was a
Philadelphian who led the Grand Army of the Republic at the beginning of the Civil War. Another Civil War hero is memorialized in a
statue here; **Major General John Fulton Reynolds** (John Rogers, 1884)
was killed by a sharpshooter at Gettysburg.

Frank Rizzo is the larger-than-life fellow raising his hand as if to hail
a taxi on the opposite side of Arch Street. Rizzo was police commis-

sioner and mayor of Philadelphia in the tumultuous 1970s and was both revered and reviled during his career. This sculpture, by Zenos Frudakis, was installed in 1998.

Rizzo had a stormy relationship with the city's proponents of the arts. The sculpture to the former mayor's left, your right, is **Government of the People** by Jacques Lipchitz. It was installed here in 1976 during Rizzo's tenure as mayor. Rizzo once described it as a load of plaster dropped from a plasterer's hawk. Lipchitz describes it as a representation of democracy, continual struggle, and mutual support, resulting in ultimate victory. A family of three on the bottom support a younger and an older couple rising above.

Farther to your right is **Benjamin Franklin, Craftsman,** by Joseph Brown. It was installed in 1981 by the Freemasons of Pennsylvania on their 250th anniversary. Brown was blind in one eye and losing vision in the other when he created this piece.

The **Masonic Temple** (Tu–F tours at 11, 2, and 3, Sa, tours at 10 and 11) is the white building on the right at the corner of Broad and Filbert Streets. It was built by James Windrim from 1868 to 1873 in Romanesque Revival style. George Herzog did the interiors for the elaborate theme rooms based on historic buildings such as the Alhambra and the Temple of Luxor.

The first Freemason Temple in America was founded in 1732. Today's Freemasons are the distant offspring of the old artisan guilds of Europe. Medieval masons were not only bricklayers, they were also engineers, designers, and architects. The men who knew how to build the great medieval churches and castles were rich and powerful. Knowledge was carefully guarded to protect guild members and no outsiders were allowed to see manuscripts or plans. During the English Reformation, the king confiscated the property of all guild members, forcing them to retreat into total secrecy to protect their wealth. As the flames of the Reformation cooled and knowledge began to spread both with and without consent, many guilds simply faded away. Masons,

MASONIC HALL, BROAD AND JUNIPER STREETS ☞

however, their ran
famous a
found th
increased
ety mem
describe t

You ca
This is pr
to the cha
Oldenbur
itarian ite
and findin
was holdin
Pennsylva

Triune,
the square
sity of Pen
sion by F
Engman re
was comm
gation to t
to the city
ect.

William
stands on t
nated in 19
public subs
sen but die
statue.

6.35 Leave

The colorf
This not-qu
had the big

TRIUNE BY ROBERT ENGMAN, FIFTEENTH AND MARKET STREETS

1930s. They also designed the Drake Tower and the Packard Building (Tour 4).

The **Philadelphia Savings Fund Society (PSFS) Building** is on the right at Twelfth Street. Built between 1930 and 1932 by Howe and Lescaze, this is one of Philadelphia's architectural treasures. Now a hotel, the building was the first International-style skyscraper in America, and its sweeping lines of stainless steel and polished granite have been copied many times.

6.7   Right on Tenth Street.

St. Stephen's Protestant Episcopal Church is on the left, built on one of the spots reputed to be where Ben Franklin flew his kite. This was designed in 1822 in Gothic style by William Strickland. Frank Furness added the north transepts in 1878. On the right just before Chestnut Street is the beautiful **Victory Building**, designed by Henry Fernbach in 1873 in Second Empire style. This building was neglected for many years and was slated for demolition. The relentless efforts of concerned citizens and historical preservationists finally succeeded when Thomas Jefferson University assumed control of the building in the late 1990s, renovated it, and began using it for university housing in 2003.

6.8   Left on Chestnut Street.

Franklin Parkway architect Paul Philippe Cret designed the **Federal Reserve Bank** on Tenth and Chestnut Streets in 1931. It is a classical design with modern sensibility, including two Art Deco reliefs on the sides of the main entrance.

6.85 Left on Ninth Street.

The **United States Post Office and Court House** is on the left, built from 1934 to 1940 in Art Deco style by Harry Sternfield, a student of Paul Philippe Cret, who designed the Parkway and the Ben Franklin Bridge. Check out the stylized postal workers in the carvings on the side. The four Art Deco reliefs, called *Mail Delivery,* were created from 1934 to 1940 by Edmond Amaties.

7.0   End at Ninth and Market Streets.

ATTRACTIONS AROUND CITY HALL

City Hall, Broad and Market Streets, Visitor Center in Room 121 (215) 686-2840, M–F 9:30–4:15, self-guided tower tours, one-hour interior tour 12:30, free.

Eastern State Penitentiary, 2124 Fairmount Avenue (215) 236-3300,

June–Aug., W–Su 10–5; May and Sept.–early Nov., Sa–Su 10–5, optional guided tours on the hour and half-hour, Sa and Su P.M., last tour at 4, http://www.easternstate.org, admission.

Franklin Institute, Twentieth Street and Ben Franklin Parkway (215) 448-1200, Science Center, daily 9:30–5, Mandell Center, Su–Th 9:30–5, F–Sa 9:30–9, http://www.fi.edu, admission.

Gallery at Market East, 901 Market Street, information at (215) 625-4962, M, T, Th, Sa 10–7, W, F 10–8, Su 12–5, http://www.premier-marketplaces.com, food sales.

Masonic Temple, 1 North Broad Street, (215) 988-1900, Tu–F tours at 11, 2, and 3, Sa, tours at 10 and 11, http://www.pagrandlodge.org, free.

Pennsylvania Academy of the Fine Arts, 118 North Broad Street (215) 972-7600, fax (215) 569-0153, Tu–Sa 10–5, Su 11–5, http://www.pafa.org, admission.

Philadelphia Free Library, Central Branch, 1901 Vine Street (215) 686-5322, M–Th 9–9, F 9–6, Sa 9–5, http://www.library.phila.gov, free.

Reading Terminal Market, between Market and Arch Streets, Eleventh and Twelfth Streets (215) 922-2317, M–Sa 8–6, http://www.readingterminalmarket.org, food sales.

Rodin Museum, Twenty-second and Ben Franklin Parkway (215) 763-8100, Tu–Su 10–5, http://www.rodinmuseum.org, admission.

Rittenhouse Square and South Broad Street

DISTANCE: 5 miles, 8 km

TERRAIN: Flat. Paved roads in city traffic. You will need to walk your bike for a few short sections: three blocks on one-way streets, one block through Rittenhouse Square, and one crosswalk.

START: The **Kimmel Center for the Performing Arts** at Broad and Spruce Streets.

ACCESS BY CAR: From **I-676** take the Broad Street exit. South on Broad Street. Follow Broad around City Hall and continue south for four blocks to Spruce Street. There are parking garages in the area and parking at meters on the street.

ACCESS BY PUBLIC TRANSPORTATION: All **SEPTA Regional Rail Lines** stop at Suburban Station at Sixteenth Street and JFK Boulevard. Ride south on Fifteenth Street about five blocks to Locust Street. Turn left and ride one block to Broad Street. Turn right and ride one block to Spruce Street. The **Market/Frankford High Speed Line** stops at Fifteenth and Market Streets. Ride south on Fifteenth Street to Locust Street, about five blocks. Turn left on Locust and ride one block to Broad Street. Turn right and ride one block south to Spruce Street. Take the Walnut/Locust exit of the **Broad Street Subway**. Ride one and a half blocks south on Broad Street to Spruce Street.

SERVICES: There are several places to buy food near Rittenhouse Square (mile 2.5) and on Chestnut and Broad Streets (miles 3.2 to 3.7).

BIKE SHOPS: Frankenstein Bike Worx, 1529 Spruce Street (215) 893-

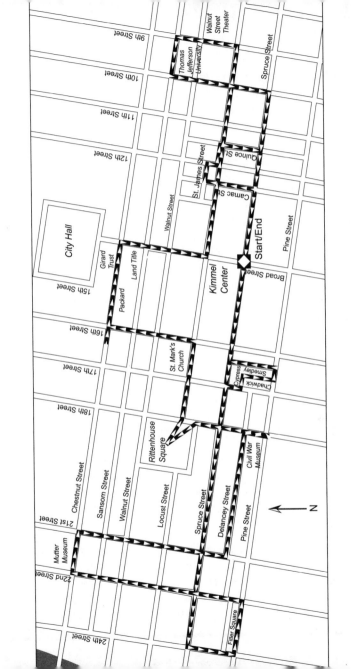

0415 (mile 0.1), and **Bicycle Therapy,** 2111 South Street (215) 735-7849 (not on route).

William Penn envisioned a grid of streets for Philadelphia. On paper, he designed five squares, named Northeast, Southeast, Northwest, Southwest, and Center, which would remain natural settings to be enjoyed by the entire populace. Penn's grid did not materialize in his lifetime, however, because the city developed north and south along the Delaware River and did not reach the Schuylkill River to the west until the early 1800s. In 1825, Southwest Square was renamed after the eighteenth-century inventor David Rittenhouse, but the first roads did not reach it until 1830, and the first house was not built on its perimeter until 1840. From that time until the present, the Rittenhouse Square neighborhood around the park has been home to many well-to-do urbanites.

The tour begins at the Kimmel Center, the new home of the Philadelphia Orchestra. Before passing the orchestra's old home, the Academy of Music, you will see Rittenhouse Square, some of Philadelphia's most elegant nineteenth-century homes, one of America's oldest theaters, some of Philadelphia's smallest residential streets, and a few historic social clubs.

0.0   Start at the corner of Spruce and Broad Streets. On street signs for Broad Street you will also see the new appellation Avenue of the Arts. From the Academy of the Fine Arts two blocks north of City Hall to the University of the Arts on Pine Street, Broad Street has a long history of theaters and fine arts education.

The **Kimmel Center for the Performing Arts** opened in December 2001. The block-long building with a glass barrel vault 150 feet above the sidewalk was designed by Rafael Viñoly and cost more than $265 million to build. During the 1990s, the Philadelphia Orchestra was looking for a new home; at the same time, Mayor Edward Rendell made the development of the Avenue of the Arts a top priority and was prepared to help the orchestra build a grand new performing arts center on Broad Street. The center houses two concert halls and is now the home of the Philly Pops Orchestra, the Chamber Orchestra of Philadelphia, and Philadanco, the region's preeminent dance performance group, and it also hosts a wide variety of guest performers. Verizon Hall seats 2,500 people in its cello-shaped hall.

South of the Kimmel Center is the **University of the Arts,** a Greek Revival building designed in 1820 by John Haviland for the Philadelphia Asylum for the Deaf and Dumb. The University of the Arts began as two separate institutions: the Pennsylvania Museum and School of Industrial Art, and the Philadelphia Musical Academy. Planners of the 1876 Centennial Exposition in Philadelphia (Tour 6) designed Memorial Hall in West Fairmount Park to display art during the exposition and then to house a permanent museum and art school. Even before the centennial's opening day, however, Memorial Hall was too small for the art collection, let alone a school, and classes were held in other locations in Center City. Named the Philadelphia Museum School of Art, the school moved to this location on Broad Street in 1893. It separated from the museum in 1964, when the name changed to the Philadelphia College of Art. The Philadelphia Musical Academy, founded in 1870, became an independent college in 1950 and took the name Philadelphia College of Performing Arts in 1976. The two colleges joined in 1985, becoming the Philadelphia College of the Arts, and then in 1987 it became the University of the Arts.

Ride west on Spruce Street toward Fifteenth Street.

You will pass the **Drake Hotel** on the left at 1512 Spruce Street, built in 1929 by Ritter and Shay (Tour 3). In the 1920s, zoning ordinances were imposed in many urban areas, requiring the top floors of skyscrapers to be recessed, which would allow more light to reach the street. As a result, many tall buildings acquired a peaked top, like the Drake Tower. Be sure to look at the terra-cotta reliefs. They have a nautical motif, in honor of namesake Sir Francis Drake. Today the building is divided into co-ops.

0.25 Left on Seventeenth Street.

0.28 Next left on **Cypress Street**.

William Penn, in his ideal on paper, divided Philadelphia into large plots of land in the hope that there would be one house on each with plenty of room for gardens and farms. Many plots were subdivided into increasingly tiny blocks, however, with several small houses along narrow alleys for the people who worked in nearby mansions. Today they are quiet oases for upscale urbanites looking for old-world charm.

0.3 Follow the road to the right onto Chadwick Street.

0.35 Left on Pine Street.

0.4 Left on Smedley Street.

0.5 Left on Spruce Street.

The **Tenth Presbyterian Church** is located on the southwest corner of Seventeenth and Spruce Streets. It was built in 1854 by John MacArthur, Jr., architect for City Hall, who was a member of the congregation.

Some of the nicest **Victorian brownstone**s in Philadelphia are found on Spruce Street between Twentieth and Twenty-second Streets. Brownstone was a popular building material during the last half of the nineteenth century because it was inexpensive and easy to carve. It was discontinued, however, in the 1880s, when it was discovered that the stone crumbles easily. Though some of these homes show signs of wear and weather damage, they nevertheless still demonstrate brownstone's decorative possibilities.

1.1 Left on Twenty-fourth Street.

1.2 Left on Pine Street.

The small park on the left is **Fitler Square**, named for Edwin Henry Fitler, the first mayor of Philadelphia to have an office in City Hall. Fitler rose to fame and fortune in the production of twine. He invented a machine that baled hay with twine instead of wire, reducing injury to workers and livestock.

1.3   Left on Twenty-second Street.

In 1890, **Wilson Eyre** designed the huge twin house at 315–317 South Twenty-second Street, on the right between Pine and Spruce Streets. Keep this house in mind when you see Eyre's flamboyant houses on Thirteenth and Locust Streets later on this tour. The simplified lines and scaled-down decoration shows the changes in design styles from high Victorian Gothic to Arts and Crafts.

Another Eyre house, built in 1889, is on the corner of Twenty-second and Chestnut Streets. Eyre put much thought into the main door of his houses, because it is where residents and guests view the exterior most frequently and most closely. Eyre's designs for residences in Philadelphia brought the city national attention.

The **Mutter Museum** (M–Sa 10–4, Su 12–4) is on this corner on the right, on the opposite side of Chestnut Street. The museum is part of the College of Physicians of Philadelphia, and its mission is to document the history of medicine in America. But its most noted collection consists of photos, castings, and preserved specimens of bizarre human abnormalities, a medical freak show of sorts.

1.7   Right on Chestnut Street.

The **First Unitarian Church** is on the left at 2125 Chestnut Street. The first Unitarian congregation in North America was established in Philadelphia in 1796. By the 1880s the church had grown and required a new building, which was dedicated in 1886 and has been altered several times. The first Unitarian Church was founded in London in 1774, dedicated to religious diversity and espousing the belief that the teachings of Jesus were more important than His divinity. Another theology, Universalism, originated in America and is based on the belief that all people would "return to God," as opposed to the belief that only a few would be saved. The two religions merged in 1961. Today, the First Unitarian Church is an active member of the Unitarian-Universalist Association.

1.75   Right on Twenty-first Street.

The **Thomas Hockley House** is on the left at 235 Twenty-first Street, between Locust and Walnut Streets. It was designed by Frank Furness in 1875, when he was just rising to prominence. The elaborate brickwork and carvings at the entrance are typical of Furness's style. He also used many natural motifs in exaggerated proportions like the flower carved above entry. There are many other houses along this street with interesting doorways and other architectural details.

235 SOUTH TWENTY-FIRST STREET, DESIGNED BY FRANK FURNESS

2.1 Left on Delancey Place.

Nobel Prize–winning novelist **Pearl S. Buck** lived in the house at 2019 on the left.

The **Rosenbach Museum and Library** (Tu, Th, F 11–4, W 11–8, Sa–Su 10-5) is on the same block on the right at 2008-2010 Delancey. This was the home of Dr. A. S. W. Rosenbach, who, with his brother Philip H. Rosenbach, dealt in rare books. It has been a museum of rare books and manuscripts since 1954. The vast collection includes the only known first edition of Franklin's *Poor Richard's Almanac* and the original copy of *Ulysses* by James Joyce. The Rosenbach brothers also collected antiques, and there is an impressive display of art and furnishings, including a gate made by master wrought iron artist Samuel Yellin.

Ride slowly along the next two blocks of **Delancey Place** to enjoy the nineteenth-century townhouses. There are interesting carvings on many windows and doorways, and you will see splendid fanlights and leaded glass. The house at 1837 was once the home of Civil War general **George Gordon Meade.**

2.35 Right on Eighteenth Street.

Walk your bike one block to Pine Street.

2.37 Walk to the right on Pine Street.

The **Civil War Library and Museum** (Th–Sa 11–4:30) is on the right, the second building from the corner. The museum was founded in 1896 amid a strong movement across the country for Civil War memorials. The Lincoln room is devoted to the memory of the assassinated president. General Meade is also well represented. You can see the stuffed head of his horse, Old Baldy, in a glass case. The long-suffering animal was wounded five times during the war but outlived the general and died at the ripe old age of thirty. The museum was started by veterans of the Union Army who donated their own possessions. Though this led to a rather meager collection of Confederate artifacts, you can see a dressing gown owned by Jefferson Davis that was in his possession as he fled the Union Army. At the time, the Northern press had a field day and reported that he was impersonating a woman in an attempt to evade capture.

2.38 Turn around and go back to Eighteenth Street.

2.4 Left on Eighteenth Street.

The **Philadelphia Art Alliance** is on the right in one tenth of a mile at 251 Eighteenth Street, opposite the southeast corner of Rittenhouse Square. The building was the home of Samuel Price Wetherill, designed in 1909 by Frank Miles Day. Wetherill's daughter Christine Wetherill Stevenson founded the Art Alliance in 1915 and moved it to this building in 1926. The alliance seeks to support emerging as well as established visual, literary, and performing artists. There are exhibits, performances, and shows open to the public, as well as opportunities for artists to gather for support and education.

On the left is **Rittenhouse Square**. If Ben Franklin was the Einstein of his age, David Rittenhouse was the Thomas Edison. Born in 1732, he was a self-educated inventor, astronomer, and clockmaker, at a time when precise measuring instruments were rare and valuable. Rittenhouse's skill in using his instruments was as great as his skill in creating them. He participated in the establishment of the Mason-Dixon Line, the most important surveying project of the time. He also built the first telescope in America and used it to become one of the first people to view the atmosphere on Venus. Rittenhouse made clocks, barometers, and hygrometers, and he was the first person to use a spider's web as crosshairs on a telescope.

The first roads from the Delaware River to Rittenhouse Square were built in the 1830s, and the first house was completed in 1840. The park's central plaza, entrance, fountain, and pool were designed by Paul Philippe Cret, who also designed the Franklin Parkway and the Franklin Bridge. The area quickly became popular with wealthy Philadelphians and continued to attract affluent residents even as the upper classes began to move out of the city in the 1920s. By the 1950s, many private houses were razed, and luxury hotels and apartment

**RITTENHOUSE SQUARE,
EIGHTEENTH AND
LOCUST STREETS**

buildings took their place. The area surrounding Rittenhouse Square
has the distinction of being the only Philadelphia neighborhood that
has always been prosperous.

Walk your bike through the middle of the park. The bronze sculpture *Lion Crushing a Serpent* was created in 1832 by Antoine Louis
Barye. Barye was one of the first nineteenth-century Paris artists to pre-
fer to use animals instead of people in his sculpture and to cast in

bronze rather than carve from marble. During his lifetime he was considered a radical, but after his death his style grew in popularity in Europe and the United States. The sculpture of the goat, *Billy*, by Albert Laessle, dates to 1914 and was influenced by the movement Barye began.

The fountain, designed by Cret, in the center of the square was dismantled after World War I and restored in 2000. The statue standing in the fountain, *Duck Girl* was created by Paul Manship in 1911.

Holy Trinity Church is at the northwest corner of the square. It was designed by John Notman between 1857 and 1859. Notman was born in Scotland and became an important nineteenth-century American architect; he was a founding member of the American Institute of Architects. He also designed St. Mark's Church, which you will see later on this tour.

The last remaining Victorian mansions of the many that once surrounded the square are on the southwest corner. One of the residents along this street, Henry P. McIlhenny, amassed an art collection valued at $50 million and bequeathed it to the Philadelphia Museum of Art in 1986. He lived at **1914 South Rittenhouse Square.**

2.75 Ride east on Locust Street from Eighteenth Street.

The **Curtis Institute of Music** is on the right on the corner of Eighteenth and Locust Streets. One of the foremost music institutes in the country, it was founded by Mary Louise Curtis Bok Zimbalist. She was the daughter of Cyrus H. K. Curtis, who built the successful Curtis Publishing Company (Tour 1). Conductor Efrem Zimbalist was Mary Louise's second husband and one of the institute's first instructors. The building was originally the home of George Childs Drexel, son of financier Anthony J. Drexel (Tour 10).

There are more Victorian townhouses on these next two blocks. The house at **1619 Locust Street** was the site of the rare book shop owned by the Rosenbach brothers.

On the opposite side of Locust Street, the mansion to the left of the church was once owned by Harry K. Thaw, renowned for an early twentieth-century love triangle. Thaw was married to sixteen-year-old actress and famed beauty Evelyn Nesbit, who was the mistress of architect Stanford White. When Thaw learned of the affair, he shot White to death on top of Madison Square Garden. The trial received massive public attention, becoming the first of many "trials of the century." Thaw was sentenced to life in a hospital for the criminally insane.

Next door, **St. Mark's Church** is architect John Notman's tribute to religious Gothic style and was completed in 1851. Gothic Revival is sometimes considered to be the highest form of architecture for churches, as it carries one up to God on its lofty spires. The ironwork on the doors was wrought by Samuel Yellin. You will see more of his work in a few blocks, on the Packard Building on Chestnut Street.

2.9   Left on Sixteenth Street.

3.1   Walk on the sidewalk to the left on Chestnut Street.

Walk about a half-block to the 1928 Art Deco **WCAU Building** at 1620 Chestnut Street, named for the radio station it was once home to. The studio was in a glass tower and was lit up in blue at night during broadcasts. It was renovated in 1983 for the **Art Institute of Philadelphia,** still in residence here.

3.15   Turn around and ride east on Chestnut Street. Bicycles share the
      right lane with buses.

The **bus stop shelters** on Chestnut Street are works of art themselves. They were designed by Pablo Tauler and were constructed in 2000.

The **Packard Building** is on the right at Fifteenth Street. The best parts of this building are the ironwork lighting fixtures and ten-ton gates made by Samuel Yellin in 1924. Yellin was born in 1885 in Poland, where he trained as a blacksmith. He emigrated to Philadelphia in 1905 and enrolled in classes at the Pennsylvania Museum and School of Industrial Art (now the University of the Arts). His skill level already exceeded that of his instructors, so he was hired as a teacher. By the time of his death in 1940, Yellin was internationally recognized as the greatest modern master of hand-wrought iron. However, his work became less popular as sleek modern styles replaced the intricate designs of Art Nouveau and Art Deco.

The next building is the **Jacob Reed's Sons Store**, also on the right, built in 1903 in the style of an urban Italian palace. Take a look at the entryway. Inside the arch between the Corinthian pillars you will see handmade tiles by **Henry Chapman Mercer**, a practitioner of the Arts and Crafts style.

Look up for the best view of the **Crozer Building**, next on the right. There is a French chateau on top of this tall commercial building designed by Frank Miles Day in 1898.

The **Girard Trust Company**, now the **Ritz-Carlton Hotel**, is on the left just before Broad Street. It was built between 1905 and 1908 as a modern Pantheon. The building is a combination of classical design and modern technology. The façade is white Georgia marble, but the underlying structure is steel.

3.5   Right on Broad Street.

The **Land Title Buildings**, on this block on the right, were designed by D. H. Burnham and Company in 1897 and 1902. Daniel Burnham built many early skyscrapers in Chicago in this Beaux-Arts and Neo-classical Revival style. The Land Title Company is the oldest title insurance company in the world.

The **Union League** is also on the right just past Sansom Street. The league was founded in 1862 to support President Lincoln's war policies in the face of growing pro-Southern sentiment in the city. Visiting Philadelphia in 1864, Lincoln was impressed with the Union League and promised to attend the grand opening of the new building the following year, but he was assassinated before the event took place. The opening was canceled, and the building was draped in black while Lincoln's body lay in state in Independence Hall.

The league is active today with three thousand members and more than eighty events a year. Admission was originally granted to anyone professing complete loyalty to the Union and promising to eschew

GIRARD TRUST AND THE LAND TITLE BUILDING, CHESTNUT AND BROAD 🖝
STREETS

nonunionists. Today, membership is by invitation only and reserved for the social elite.

There are two statues of American soldiers in front of the Union League. The one with the stovepipe hat, from 1872, is **Washington Grays Monument** by J. Wilson. The soldier with the rifle over his shoulder is *Spirit of '61* by Henry Kirke Bush-Brown and was created in 1911.

The **Bellevue** is also on the right, just past Walnut Street. When it was constructed between 1902 and 1913, the entire building was the Bellevue-Stratford Hotel and was one of the grandest hotels in America. The deaths of twenty-nine members of the American Legion in 1976 due to contaminated air conditioning units led to its swift and almost irrevocable decline. Today, the **Park Hyatt Hotel** is located on the upper floors and much of the building is used as commercial office space. The **Shops at the Bellevue** include some very pricey restaurants but also a less expensive gourmet food court.

The **Academy of Music** is on the southwest corner of Locust and Broad Streets. Napoleon Le Brun and Gustav Runge based the building's design on La Scala in Milan, Italy. It opened on January 26, 1857, and is the oldest concert hall and opera house in the country. It was the home of the Philadelphia Orchestra from its inception in 1900 until 2001, when the orchestra moved to the Kimmel Center just to the south. The academy is still the home of the Pennsylvania Ballet, and there is still a full calendar of events.

The **Merriam Theater** is also on the right and the **Wilma Theater** is on the left. The Merriam was originally called the Shubert Theater; built in 1918, it was constructed to seat almost seventeen hundred people. It was renamed in 1991 for John W. Merriam, an active supporter for the development of the Avenue of the Arts and a benefactor of the University of the Arts, the theater's owner. Traveling productions of Broadway musicals frequently stop at the Merriam. In contrast, the three-hundred-seat Wilma Theater was built in 1994 (the first professional theater built in Center City since 1928) and is Philadelphia's most noted experimental theater company. The Wilma moved to this location after sixteen years in a tiny theater near Rittenhouse Square.

3.7 Left on Locust Street. You will need to dismount your bike and make this turn in the crosswalk because left turns are prohibited for vehicular traffic.

There are two houses designed by Wilson Eyre on the left on the next block. The first, at **1321 Locust Street,** was built in 1890, earlier than the Eyre houses you passed on Twenty-first and Twenty-second Streets. Next door, the house at **1319 Locust Street** was built three years later in a Victorian version of Georgian Revival.

The **Library Company of Philadelphia** (M–F 9–4:45) is on the right at 1314 Locust Street. Founded by Benjamin Franklin in 1731, the original building was located behind Independence Hall. The marble sculpture of **Franklin** in the window of this building was carved by Francesco Lazzarini in 1789. It was displayed outside of the Library Company's first building but was damaged by exposure and moved to several indoor locations before it was installed here. Franklin is wearing an eighteenth-century shirt, but he is also draped in a toga. The early Americans, who idealized ancient Greece, used Greek symbols and designs frequently.

Also on the right, the **Historical Society of Pennsylvania** (Tu, Th, F 9:30–4, W 1–8, Sa 10–4) is at 1300 Locust Street. Founded in 1824, the society moved to this building in 1901.

You will pass **Thomas Jefferson University** at Tenth and Locust Streets. The university was founded in 1824 and is a private college with one of the largest independent medical schools in the country, which opened in 1877. Among its illustrious faculty was Samuel David Gross, who wrote *Elements of Pathological Anatomy*, one of the most influential medical texts in English, in 1839. Gross is portrayed in Thomas Eakins's work *The Gross Clinic*, painted in 1875. The painting was criticized at the time for its unblinking realism, but Eakins is now considered one of America's greatest painters, and this painting, owned by and displayed in Jefferson University, is considered by many to be his masterpiece. You can see the painting in the Eakins Gallery in the Jefferson Alumni Hall, between Tenth and Eleventh Streets on Locust Street (M–Sa 10–4, Su 12–4).

4.1   Left on Ninth Street.

The **Wills Eye Institute** has a building completed in 2002 on the right at Walnut and Ninth Streets. In front of the building stands one of my favorite works of art in the city: *Starman in the Ancient Garden* by Brower Hatcher. The starman is crashing down to Earth with bits and pieces of civilization trapped in his cometlike tail. Landing amid the scattered remnants of ancient culture, the look on his face is serene.

On the opposite side of Walnut Street is the **Walnut Street Theater,** designed by John Haviland (Tour 1) in Greek Revival style. It opened in 1809 and is the oldest continuously used theater in the country.

**STARMAN IN THE ANCIENT
GARDEN BY BROWER HATCHER,
NINTH AND WALNUT STREETS**

Almost every famous American nineteenth- and twentieth-century stage actor has performed here along with many notable foreign actors. It is one of the best respected theaters in the country.

4.25 Left on Sansom Street.

4.35 Left on Tenth Street.

4.55 Right on Spruce Street.

4.75 Walk to the right on **Camac Street,** which is one-way coming toward you.

The **Philadelphia Inn** is on the right in one block. This is at least the third restaurant on this site, going back to the early 1800s, when Camac Street was part of the city's Latin Quarter and was lined with bordellos and taverns. The Inn is now a highly rated restaurant.

After an energetic campaign to rid the area of prostitution and drunkenness, Camac became known as the street of little clubs. The club movement started in the mid-1800s, primarily as a way for women with similar interests to meet. As more women began to study and work in what had been men's arenas, they felt the need for support and socialization. The clubs were usually modest in means and membership, and Camac Street's small and newly vacated buildings provided inexpensive venues.

The **Plastic Club** at 247 Camac is on the right, just past the Inn. It was founded in 1897 for women artists and is still in operation. The **Philadelphia Sketch Club** at 235 Camac is also on the right at the end of the same block. It is the oldest professional artists' club in the country, founded in 1860 by Pennsylvania Academy students. The **Franklin Club,** 205 Camac, is on the corner of St. James and Camac Streets. It is a private literary club founded in 1902.

Stop a moment before turning onto St. James Street to look at the wooden paving blocks on Camac Street in the next block. This type of pavement was common in the early 1800s, but today Camac is the only street in America still paved in wood. The blocks were perfect for travel by horse but are not suitable for auto traffic and need regular maintenance. In the 1980s city officials wanted to replace them with sturdier materials; however, local residents lobbied in favor of keeping the wood and persuaded the city to keep this one block in historical condition.

4.9   Right on St. James Street.

4.95   Right on Twelfth Street.

5.0   Left on Locust Street.

5.1   Right on Quince Street.

Quince Street is part of a charming warren of residential streets and is similar to Chadwick and Smedley Streets, which you passed on this tour.

5.2   Right on Spruce Street.

5.35   End at Spruce and Broad Streets.

ATTRACTIONS AROUND RITTENHOUSE SQUARE AND SOUTH BROAD STREET

Civil War Library and Museum, 1805 Pine Street (215) 735-8196, Th–Sa 11–4:30, admission.

Historical Society of Pennsylvania, 1300 Locust Street (215) 732-6200, Tu, Th, F 9:30–4, W 1–8, Sa 10–4, http://www.hsp.org, admission.

Library Company of Philadelphia, 1314 Locust Street (215) 546-3181, M–F 9–4:45, free.

Mutter Museum, College of Physicians of Philadelphia, 19 South Twenty-second Street (215) 563-3737, M–Sa 10–4, Su 12–4, http://www.collphyphil.org, admission.

Rosenbach Museum and Library, 2008-2010 Delancey Place (215) 732-1600, Tu, Th, F 11–4, W 11–8, Sa–Su 10–5, http://www.rosen-bach.org, admission.

East Fairmount Park

DISTANCE: 9.5 miles, 15.4 km

TERRAIN: The first half is on roads with light traffic except two sections on Thirty-third Street (0.3 mile) and Ridge Avenue (1.3 miles), where traffic is heavier. At the end of both of these you will need to make a left turn, but there are traffic lights and you can walk one or both in the crosswalks. There are also two long hills and a few short ones. The second half is flat and on a paved bike path.

START: Behind the Philadelphia Museum of Art on Aquarium and Kelly Drives.

ACCESS BY CAR: From I-676 to the Art Museum/Franklin Parkway/Twenty-second Street exit. Follow signs to the parkway. Turn left and follow the signs for the museum. You will leave Eakins Oval, the traffic circle in front of the museum, on Kelly Drive just before the circle passes in front of the museum. Turn left at the second light, Aquarium Boulevard, just before the first boat house. There is free parking along this street.

ACCESS BY PUBLIC TRANSPORTATION: All **SEPTA Regional Rail Lines** stop at Suburban Station. Ride from the northwest corner of the station on the Franklin Parkway toward the art museum to Twenty-second Street, about half a mile. Turn right. In one block, turn left on Pennsylvania Avenue. Ride about half a mile to Twenty-fifth Street. Turn left and cross Kelly Drive at the traffic light on Twenty-fifth Street. Turn right on the bike path. Ride one-tenth of a mile and turn left on Aquarium Drive. The **Market/Frankford** and **Broad Street High Speed Lines** stop at Fifteenth and Market Streets. Ride one block west on Market Street and turn right on Sixteenth Street. Ride two blocks north, and turn left on the Franklin Parkway. Go northwest

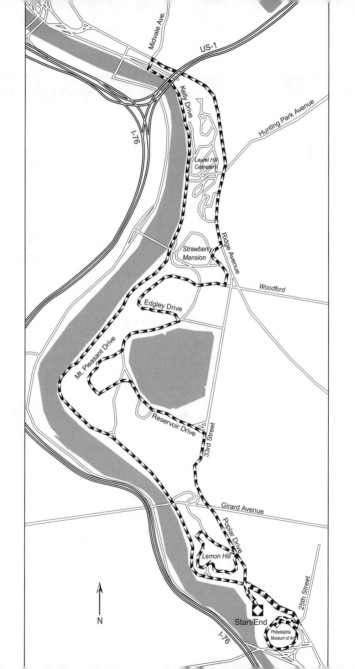

Midvale Ave.

US-1

I-76

Kelly Drive

Hunting Park Avenue

(Laurel Hill) Cemetery

Ridge Avenue

Strawberry Mansion

Woodford

Edgley Drive

Mt. Pleasant Drive

Reservoir Drive

33rd Street

Girard Avenue

Poplar Drive

Lemon Hill

25th Street

N

Start/End

Philadelphia Museum of Art

I-76

PHILADELPHIA MUSEUM OF ART, EAKINS OVAL ON THE BENJAMIN FRANKLIN PARKWAY on the Parkway toward the art museum to Twenty-second Street, about half a mile. Turn right. In one block, turn left on Pennsylvania Avenue. Ride about half a mile to Twenty-fifth Street. Turn left and cross Kelly Drive at the traffic light on Twenty-fifth Street. Turn right on the bike path. Ride one-tenth of a mile and turn left on Aquarium Drive. Take the City Hall exit from the **Broad Street Subway**. Ride west on Market Street two blocks and turn right on Sixteenth Street. Ride two blocks north, and turn left on the Franklin Parkway. Go northwest on the Parkway toward the art museum to Twenty-second Street, about half a mile. Turn right. In one block, turn left on Pennsylvania Avenue. Ride about half a mile to Twenty-fifth Street. Turn left and cross Kelly Drive at the traffic light on Twenty-fifth Street. Turn right on the bike path. Ride one-tenth of a mile, and turn left on Aquarium Drive.

SERVICES: Snacks at Lloyd Hall, restaurant in the Philadelphia Museum of Art (near the start), convenience store at Ridge Avenue and Midvale Avenue (mile 5.5).

BIKE SHOPS: Drive Sports, 2601 Pennsylvania Avenue (215) 232-7368 (near the start) and **Cycle Sport,** 2329 Brown Street (215) 765-9100 (not on route).

With sixty-five parks scattered throughout the city on almost nine thousand acres, no Philadelphia resident lives more than a mile from Fairmount Park. The largest city park in the country and one of Philadelphia's greatest assets, it grew indirectly out of the Fairmount Water Works, an early nineteenth-century technological wonder and internationally renowned public garden. This tour begins at the Water Works, standing in the shadow of the Philadelphia Museum of Art. You will then ride past several colonial era houses on the bluffs above the Schuylkill River. These estates, now part of Fairmount Park, were once the summer country homes of some of Philadelphia's wealthy residents including two men who signed the Declaration of Independence and a privateer engaged by the provisional government to plunder British ships. Most of the mansions are furnished with period pieces and are open to the public for tours. Riding back down to the river on the second half of the route, you will see some of the artwork acquired and installed in the park over the past 130 years by the Fairmount Art Association before you return to the Museum of Art and the Water Works.

0.0   Begin at the newly renovated **Fairmount Water Works.**

By the end of the American Revolution, Philadelphia was a rapidly growing city, the largest and wealthiest in the nation. It was also plagued with overcrowding, poverty, filthy streets, and clogged sewers. Physicians of the time recognized the importance of abundant clean water for drinking and washing to reduce the spread of such diseases as yellow fever, which crippled Philadelphia in 1793.

At the turn of the nineteenth century, a pumping station was built in Center Square where City Hall stands today, but by 1812 it was inadequate to meet the needs of the expanding population.

The city bought five acres of land on the Schuylkill River just below Fairmount, the current location of the Philadelphia Museum of Art and the highest land on the edge of the city. Frederick Graff, water commissioner from 1805 to 1847, designed the new water works to pump water from the river into a reservoir on Fairmount. When it opened, Philadelphia residents were the recipients of running water decades before the rest of the country.

The first design, operational in 1815, used two state-of-the-art steam engines housed in a Federal-style mansion to pump water into the reservoir. The cutting edge technology was unfortunately not yet perfected. In 1819, after two explosions and at least one death, the more traditional method of a dam and water wheels was used to pump river water to the reservoir. At the time, the dam was the longest in the world. The sixteen-foot-diameter wheels were enclosed in Greek Revival arcades with viewing galleries, creating a temple to human technology.

Graff surrounded the water works with elaborate formal gardens that included fountains, gazebos, and statues. At the time, Americans were afraid of the power of unbridled nature as well as the dangers of the cities. The Fairmount Water Works and gardens seemed to epitomize man's ability to control his environment for his own benefit.

Thousands of people from the United States and Europe visited this shrine to human ingenuity. Hotels and restaurants were built to accommodate the spectators, including a restaurant in the main pump house. Additionally, the slow-moving pool created behind the dam was perfect for boating. Excursion steamboats began to carry visitors up and down the river, and the sport of rowing became popular. The Water Works became the second most popular tourist attraction in America after Niagara Falls.

Look above the water works at the two white statues by William Rush. *River Chained*, on the right, is a miserable savage, and *River Freed*, on the left, is a contented, civilized lady. By damming the river, controlling its flow, and harnessing its power for human use, we have "freed" the river.

Graff's son, Frederic Graff, Jr., took over as water commissioner after the senior Graff's death in 1847, but he lacked his father's vision. The Water Works were expanded in the 1860s but no filters were added to purify the raw water, now polluted by upstream mills. Philadelphia experienced an epidemic of typhoid fever in the 1890s, and unfiltered water from the Schuylkill River was a major source of contamination. The city attempted to control the water quality by purchasing some of the estates just upstream from the Water Works, but poor water quality combined with demand for more output and an increasing population caused the permanent closure of the facility in 1909.

An aquarium was then built on the site and remained in operation until 1962, although the general condition of the grounds and buildings declined over the years. A public swimming pool replaced the aquarium for about ten years before the area was fenced off and more or less abandoned. Today, a projected $5 million restoration of the Water Works is under way, and the pump house is planned to become a restaurant once again.

Cross Reservoir Drive where the name of the road
o Dauphin Drive.

Man by Cyrus E. Dallin (1899) is on the left on Dauphin
as raised in Utah, where his father owned a mine. As a
oft white clay near the mine and modeled human heads
kill that his family enrolled him in art school. Eventu-
:o Paris to study and saw Buffalo Bill's Wild West Show.
drew him back to his youth in Utah, and he began to
celebrated American Indians. The Fairmount Park Art
talled this work here in 1903.

nt Park Art Association was established in 1872 with
exel (Tour 10) as its first president. It is dedicated to
city planning and has commissioned or purchased most
ublic viewing in the park. Philadelphia has more public
her city in North America, largely because of the Fair-
rt Association and the efforts of the Redevelopment

Strawberry Mansion Drive in front of the **Woodford**
(Tu–Su 10–4).

built as a one-story house on land bought by William
56. Coleman's nephew, George Clymer, who signed the
Independence, sold it to Alexander Barclay in 1769.
to his brother-in-law David Franks in 1771. Franks
ess of enlarging Woodford by building odd-sized addi-
r of the main section.

pted to be on both sides of the Revolution. He signed the
on Agreement of 1765, agreeing not to buy goods from
e Stamp Act was repealed. But he was also a Tory who
ny in British high society here before and during the
on of Philadelphia. He was arrested for treason by Bene-
10 was later arrested for the same crime. Woodford was
d Franks was exiled to New York in 1780. The house

0.1 Exit the Water Works and follow the circle around the **Seahorse Fountain** toward Kelly Drive.

This is a 1926 replica of the 1740 Fontana dei Cavalli Marini in the Villa Borghese gardens in Rome and was a gift to the United States from the Italian government. It arrived in Philadelphia in seventy-six pieces and was reassembled by Italian craftsmen.

0.25 Cross Kelly Drive at the light onto Poplar Drive.

After Abraham Lincoln was assassinated, the city was eager to erect a monument to him. Over $22,000 was raised in a year and Randolph Rogers was commissioned to create the statue of **Lincoln** signing the Emancipation Proclamation on the right. When it was installed on May 22, 1865, fifty thousand people attended.

0.45 Hard left on Lemon Hill Drive.

In 1770, Robert Morris, who later signed the Declaration of Independence and helped finance the American Revolution, bought this land and built a farm he called the Hills. By 1799, however, Morris was bankrupt, and Henry Pratt bought at sheriff's sale forty-three acres of the Hills for a summer country estate. Pratt built **Lemon Hill** (W–Su 10–4), the Federal-style house that stands today, and created formal gardens that included the first lemon trees planted in the country. The gardens were so popular that Pratt began to charge admission. Pratt died in 1838 and his estate was bankrupt by 1840, when the Bank of the United States acquired Lemon Hill at sheriff's sale. In 1843, the city purchased the house and forty-five-acre formal garden. It was the first piece of property for what was to become Fairmount Park.

The city continued to purchase estates along the river, many of which had gardens and lawns, making the creation of a public park relatively easy. Today, Fairmount Park contains the largest collection of eighteenth- and early nineteenth-century country estates in America. There are more than two hundred buildings on about 250 acres, mostly in East and West Fairmount Park. The Pennsylvania General Assembly officially named these properties Fairmount Park in 1867, and the Fairmount Park Commission was created the next year. The park continues to acquire new land and today it encompasses almost nine thousand acres, about 10 percent of all the land within the city limits.

1.0　Right on Sedgley Drive.

On the right at this intersection is the 1881 statue of **Morton McMichael** by John Mahoney. McMichael was mayor of Philadelphia from 1866 to 1869 and the first president of the Fairmount Park Commission from 1867 to 1879.

1.2　Left on Poplar Drive.

1.5　Straight at the light, crossing Girard Avenue where Poplar Drive joins Thirty-third Street.

You will be riding on a moderately busy street for the next 0.3 mile.

1.6　Straight at the next light where Thirty-third Street joins U.S. 13.

1.9　Left at the light into East Fairmount Park. The street is Oxford Road to the right and Reservoir Drive to the left. There is a traffic light at this intersection with a green arrow for left turns. It is legal to make your turn from the left-turn lane or you can walk across the street in the pedestrian crosswalk.

Fairmount Park is well suited for many forms of recreation. There is a golf course on your left and there are six more golf courses throughout the park. There are more than one hundred ball fields, including baseball, softball, football, and soccer fields, plus grounds for cricket, field hockey, and rugby. There are also more than one hundred tennis courts, a bowling green, and three bocce courts. The six indoor recreation centers house one outdoor and three indoor pools. There are one hundred miles of bridle paths and hiking trails, and some twenty-five miles of paved bike and pedestrian paths.

2.4　Left on Mount Pleasant Drive.

2.55　Cross Fountain Green Drive.

2.6　Follow the road to the right aroun[d] Mansion (Tu–Su 10–4).

Captain John MacPherson bought this house was completed in 1765. He call[ed] Scottish home. The house and outbuild[ings] Georgian in design. The brick details in [Scot]tish Georgian style.

MacPherson was a privateer, a sanct[ion] government's blessing to plunder British He proudly and frequently announced th[at] twice. Finding retirement in the country t[oo] back to the city in 1770. The house was [Bene]dict Arnold purchased it for his bride, [but] arrested for treason before the couple co[uld]

3.0　Left on Reservoir Drive.

Ormiston Mansion (Sa–Su 11–4 in June[.] was built in 1798 by Major Edward Burd Scottish home. The style is late Georgian.

3.25　Left on Edgley Drive.

3.4　Follow the road to the right.

Rebecca Rawle, a widow with three sm[all] section of **Laurel Hill Mansion** (Tu–Su 1[0] married Samuel Shoemaker, who was may Revolution. The family needed more roo[m] the left was tacked on in the late eighteen[th] The octagon on the right was added shor[tly] to modernize the place. Rebecca died in 1[8] ited by her oldest son, William Rawle, cofounded the Philadelphia Bar Associat[ion] Laurel Hill in 1828, and it was eventua Philadelphia in 1869.

3.8　Stra[ight] cha[nge]

The Medi[a] Street. Da[...] boy, he fo[...] with so m[...] ally, he m[...] The exper[...] create art Associatio[n] The Fa[...] Anthony including of the art art than a mount Pa[rk] Authority

3.9　Left Ma[...]

Woodfor[d] Coleman Declaratio[n] Barclay s[...] began the tions to t[...] Franks Non-imp[ortation] Britain u[...] entertaine[d] British oc[...] dict Arno[ld] confiscate[d]

WOODFORD MANSION, EAST FAIRMOUNT PARK ON DAUPHIN STREET

was purchased in 1793 by Isaac Wharton, his wife, Margaret, and daughter Rebecca Rawle, who owned Laurel Hill. Woodford stayed in the Wharton family until 1868, when it was bought by the city.

4.0   Straight on **Strawberry Mansion** Drive.

Charles Thomson, secretary of the Continental Congress, bought the estate on the left and built a house around 1750. When in 1777 it was under threat of British occupation, Thomson ordered it burned.

After the war, Judge William Lewis erected the Federal-style central section between 1788 and 1789. Lewis died in 1819, and the house was sold to Judge Joseph Hemphill, president-judge of the United States District Court of Pennsylvania, who was active in Philadelphia social circles. To accommodate his guests, he added the two Greek

Revival wings in the 1820s, making it the largest house in Fairmount Park. In 1844, George Crock purchased the property and used it as a dairy farm until the city bought it in 1871.

The estate continues to the Schuylkill River, where it was the site of steamboat landings during the nineteenth century. A woman listed only as "Mrs. Grimes" rented the house and ran a restaurant catering to the steamboat passengers. It became known as Strawberry Mansion in honor of a favorite dessert made of strawberries grown on the property. It was leased as a restaurant until 1930 and is now open to the public (Tu–Su 10–4).

4.1   Right on Cumberland Drive.

4.15 Left on Ridge Avenue, U.S. 13. Ridge Avenue has moderate traffic.

The entrance to **Laurel Hill Cemetery** is on the left at 4.8 miles. John Notman designed the parklike landscape in 1836, and the cemetery was a popular place to come for walks and picnics throughout the 1800s.

At the time, to attract prosperous families, cemetery owners wanted to inter prestigious people. The owners of Laurel Hill spoke to the family of Charles Thomson, the first owner of Strawberry Mansion, who had been buried in the Harriton cemetery for fourteen years. Unanimous family approval was required to disinter Thomson and his wife, however, and one nephew remained opposed to the plans. Soon thereafter, cemetery workers saw "suspicious characters" at the Thomson graves. When the Harriton workers approached, the "grave robbers" fled, leaving behind a cart loaded with two caskets and evidence of digging at the Thomson graves. It was never established that the Thomsons had been disinterred from the Harriton graves, nor were the contents of the abandoned caskets checked. Nonetheless, the family decided to bury them in Laurel Hill. Markers for Thomson and his wife were carved, and Laurel Hill Cemetery had its first residents.

Many famous nineteenth-century Philadelphians are buried here, including Declaration of Independence–signer Thomas McKean, astronomer and clockmaker David Rittenhouse, inventor Thomas Godfrey, architect Frank Furness and his father, and Civil War heroes including General George Meade. There are also large mausoleums for many of Philadelphia's prosperous post–Civil War industrialists.

4.5   Straight where Hunting Park Avenue crosses Ridge Avenue and U.S. 13 turns right to join Hunting Park Avenue.

5.2   Straight under the twin bridges of U.S. 1.

This is East Falls, one of several mill neighborhoods that lined the Schuylkill River in the mid-1800s because of its proximity to Center City. The area has enjoyed something of a renaissance during the past few years. Originally built for the mill workers, the row houses have been recently renovated and are gaining popularity as rental units. There is also a scattering of new restaurants and clubs on Midvale Avenue.

5.45   Left at the traffic light onto Midvale Avenue. You can walk through the intersection in the crosswalk.

5.5   Cross Kelly Drive and go left on the Kelly Drive bicycle path.

At around 6.0 miles you will see another view of **Laurel Hill Cemetery,** up on the hills to your left.

At 6.5 miles there is a **stairway** on the left leading to Strawberry Mansion. On your right you will see the stairs that came up from the riverboat landing. Excursion boat passengers crossed the road, then a gravel footpath, and hiked up the hill to Strawberry Mansion for lunch.

After riding under Strawberry Mansion Bridge you will see two boathouses on the right. The first and older boathouse serves several high school and public rowing clubs as well as the Philadelphia Police Marine Division. St. Joseph's University constructed the boathouse next door in 2002.

The cherry trees bloom along this stretch of Kelly Drive in early spring. The oldest trees were a gift of the Japanese government in the 1930s.

At about 7.5 miles you will pass a statue of **John B. Kelly,** Olympic rower, successful businessman, patron of the arts, and father of Princess Grace of Monaco. Kelly Drive is named for him.

At 8.0 miles, look both directions for more public art. The sculpture *Playing Angels* is on top of slender pedestals to the right. Carl Milles sculpted five angels in 1950, and the originals are in Millesgarden in Stockholm, Sweden. Across Kelly Drive on the right is **Ulysses S. Grant,** by Daniel Chester French, commissioned by the art association in 1885. It was installed in 1897 on the anniversary of Grant's death.

At 8.4 miles you can see *Cowboy,* by Frederic Remington, on the left. Remington grew up in Ogdensburg, New York, attended the Yale School of Art, and then moved to Montana in 1880 to become a cowboy. Returning to New York in 1886, he was a successful illustrator of cowboys for several publications. He also studied sculpture and created small bronzes of cowboys. In March 1905, the art association commissioned *Cowboy*, his only full-size sculpture. He died in 1909, one year after the installation.

At 8.5 miles the **Ellen Phillips Samuel Memorial**, one of the largest personal bequests to the city, begins on the right. In her will, Ellen Phillips Samuel specified a series of sculptures along the East River Drive, today's Kelly Drive, that would embody the history of North America. Samuel was a descendant of America's first Jewish settlers, who arrived in New England in the seventeenth century. Her family has a long history of art patronage, charitable work, and patriotism. The statues were to be sculptural portraits of people who represented the average North American settler and were to be placed every two hundred feet along East River Drive, which was then a gravel footpath. By the time plans were made to commission the sculptures, East River Drive was a paved thoroughfare for automobiles, and the selection committee thought that the sculptures would go unnoticed if they were displayed as per the original plan. They decided to cluster the works in three terraces that would encourage people to stop and enter the enclosed spaces, which would allow more contemplative review of the work. At the same time, taste in sculpture also changed and more abstract forms were replacing the realistic works of the nineteenth century.

PLAYING ANGELS BY CARL MILLES, KELLY AND FOUNTAIN GREEN DRIVES

COWBOY BY FREDERIC REMINGTON, KELLY DRIVE AT THE COLUMBIA BRIDGE

In three juried exhibitions over the next twenty years, art was selected for the memorials. You will ride by the north terrace first, followed by the central and then the south terrace, and I will describe the pieces in that order.

The north terrace exhibition, held in 1949, was attended by 250,000 people who came to see 252 works of art. The theme was the inner energies of the early American settlers. The relief panels are by J. Wallace Kelly, who called them *Titles Unknown: Eye and Hand.* The four statues inside the terrace are *The Preacher* by Waldemar Raemisch, *The Poet* by Jose de Creeft, *The Scientist* by Koren der Harootian, and *The Laborer* by Ahron Ben-Shmuel. The jury committee also chose *Social Consciousness* by Jacob Epstein, but it was too large for this space and is now located at the west entrance to the museum. (You will see it later on this ride.) *The Spirit of Enterprise* by Jacques Lipchitz was located here in the 1950s, but it was moved to the central terrace in 1986.

The exhibition to provide works for the central terrace was held in 1933, and 364 works by 105 artists were displayed. The chosen theme was westward expansion. *Spanning the Continent,* by Robert Laurent, shows a pioneer couple striding purposefully with a wheel between them. Across the terrace from this couple is another couple, *Welcoming to Freedom* by Maurice Sterne. Four sculptures on square pedestals flank these two: *The Ploughman* by J.Wallace Kelly, *The Miner* by John B. Flannagan, *The Immigrant* by Heinz Warneke, and *The Slave* by Helene Sardeau. Finally, *The Spirit of Enterprise* by Jacques Lipchitz from the 1949 exhibition is located in the middle of the terrace.

Across Kelly Drive from the central terrace is the **James A. Garfield Memorial** by Augustus Saint-Gaudens. Garfield, America's twentieth president, was assassinated in 1881 after less than a year in office. This monument was installed on Memorial Day 1896. There was an elaborate pageant on the river including hundreds of thousands of electric lights lit along the river, on boats, and along bridges. Buildings were outlined with lanterns, the beginning of today's tradition of lighting the boathouses. The dedication ceremony was attended by thousands. Saint-Gaudens was one of America's finest sculptors and the first American sculptor to be acclaimed by European artists and critics. Another of his works, *The Pilgrim,* is on the left at 9 miles.

The theme for the south terrace was the settlement of the East Coast and the emergence of the United States as an independent democracy. World War II prevented European artists from participating in the 1940 exhibition, but several museums in the United States provided pieces by foreign artists. In all 431 works were displayed. The two reliefs here are *Settling of the Seaboard* by Wheeler Williams and *The Birth of a Nation* by Henry Kreiss. The four sculptures are *The Puritan* and *The Quaker,* both by Harry Rosin, and *The Revolutionary Soldier* and *The Statesman,* both by Erwin Frey.

After the third terrace you will see *Stone Age in North America* by John J. Boyle, a sculpture that is not part of the Samuel Memorial. It was installed in West Fairmount Park near Sweetbriar Mansion in 1887 and relocated here in 1985. I can't help but wonder if this was a latter-day realization that some groups had been forgotten when the Samuel Memorial committee considered the history of North America. In any case, this sculpture of an Indian woman and her children is appropriate here, representing North America's first residents.

The first piece of the Samuel Memorial, **Thorfinn Karlsefni,** is just after *Stone Age in North America* on the right.

Boathouse Row begins at this point on the right. The first boathouses were built around 1850, but none of the original buildings remain. The oldest building is from around 1860 and most were built in the 1870s and 1880s. The Schuylkill Navy is the official association for rowers in the area. It was founded in 1858 with nine rowing clubs. Two more clubs joined within a few months, but half of the groups dissolved during the Civil War. Today, there are ten rowing clubs in the Schuylkill Navy.

Two of the buildings on boathouse row are not boathouses. The first, with the lighthouse, is the **Sedgley Club,** a private social club. **Lloyd Hall** (daily 10–4, except summer M–W 10–4, Th–Su 9–5) at the end of Boathouse Row is a public recreation center with public restrooms and a snack bar.

The statue *Silenus and the Infant Bacchus* is on the left side of Kelly Drive just after Lloyd Hall. The original fourth-century B.C. marble sculpture is in the Louvre and is attributed to Praxiteles. This bronze cast was made in 1885.

The statue just before Twenty-fifth Street on the same side of Kelly Drive as the museum is **Meher** by Khoren Der Harootian. Meher was a legendary Armenian figure from the Middle Ages. Here he represents the indefatigable spirit of the Armenian people, who have suffered for millennia at the hands of foreign invaders. This work was commissioned by Armenian-American residents to commemorate Armenian martyrs and to celebrate the freedom in their new country. It was unveiled for the American Bicentennial.

9.5   Right at the light at Twenty-fifth Street.

9.55 Left into the entrance to the upper road around the museum.

The seated figure is **John Marshall,** fourth Chief Justice of the United States Supreme Court. This is the 1931 work of William Wetmore Story. Marshall served as an officer in the Continental Army and then as secretary of state for John Adams. Adams also appointed Marshall to the Supreme Court where he served for more than thirty years, becoming the first great Supreme Court justice and writing the decisions for more than five hundred cases. This work is a copy of one that stands outside the U.S. Capitol.

Social Consciousness by Jacob Epstein, originally chosen for the Samuel Memorial, dominates the area at the west entrance to the museum. The work symbolizes the tenderness of humanity and the tragedy that makes the tenderness necessary.

On the opposite side of the entrance is *Atmosphere and Environment XII* (1970) by the celebrated American sculptor Louise Nevelson. She grew up in a lumberyard in Maine, and her first artistic endeavors were constructed from bits and pieces of discarded wood.

9.7   Right to continue up and around to the front of the **Philadelphia Museum of Art** (Tu, Th–Su 10–5, W 10–8:45) facing City Hall and the Franklin Parkway.

You will pass a gilded **General Anthony Wayne,** by John Gregory (1937), just before the front of the museum. "Mad Anthony" Wayne, Pennsylvania's greatest Revolutionary War hero, participated in the battles at Brandywine and Germantown and in the siege of Yorktown.

**VIEW OF THE BENJAMIN FRANKLIN PARKWAY FROM THE PHILADELPHIA
MUSEUM OF ART**

The museum was designed by Horace Trumbauer and is based on classical Greek temples. The central temple is Corinthian and the wings are Ionic. The project's chief designer was Julian Abele, one of the first African-American architects in the country. When the project began in 1911, there was not enough money to build all three wings, so it was decided to build the outer sections first. They correctly predicted that the unfinished look would quickly generate the needed funds to complete the central section, and the museum opened in 1928.

The growth of the new museum was hampered by the Great Depression in the 1930s; however, the creation of the Works Progress Administration (WPA) provided federal funds for many institutions for the arts and allowed this museum to remain open and continue to add to its collection.

Today, the building is still incomplete, as there are figures in only one of the temple pediments. Thirteen personalities from Greek mythology occupy the triangle at the top of the north temple, on the right as you face the museum. These were sculpted by Carl Paul Jennewein in 1932. There have been several attempts to raise the money for the other pediments, but even a $1 million windfall was judged to be too small to place figures in just one pediment.

The view from the top of the museum steps is one of the best in Philadelphia and is familiar to many from the "Rocky" movies. Sylvester Stallone filmed a statue of Rocky here in the last of the series. He hoped the piece would remain here after the filming, but no such luck. The museum decided that the work was a movie prop, not art. Rocky fans need not despair, however. Rocky raises his defiant fists at the Spectrum Sports Center in South Philadelphia.

Looking toward City Hall, you will see the **Washington Monument,** a huge figure on horseback atop a granite mountain built by Rudolf Siemering in 1897 and installed here in 1928. A fund to commission a permanent monument to Washington was established in 1810 but took seventy-one years to accumulate enough money to complete the work. Siemering was an internationally prominent sculptor known for highly symbolic works. Art world lore has it that he designed a sculpture of Frederick the Great that he was unable to sell, and when he sold the commission to the Americans, Siemering supposedly simply changed the hat and the medals and called it George Washington.

Horace Trumbauer also designed the **two fountains** on either side of Washington. One is dedicated to Captain John Ericsson, inventor, engineer, and direct descendant of Viking Leif Ericsson. Captain Ericsson designed the ironclad warship the *Monitor* that won the Civil War naval battle with the Confederate ironclad *Merrimac*. Ericsson also invented other important naval devices such as the screw propeller and the underwater cannon.

The other fountain is dedicated to Eli Kirk Price, Jr. The existence of both the Parkway and museum is largely the result of Price's efforts and dedication. Price was a Fairmount Park Commissioner who led the movement to build the Benjamin Franklin Parkway. He wanted a monumental building on top of Fairmount that would be equal in stature to City Hall, standing at the opposite end of the boulevard. Kirk had no idea of what he wanted the building to house, he just wanted something grand. At the time, Philadelphia's principal art museum was Memorial Hall in West Fairmount Park (Tour 6). Opening in 1877 as the Pennsylvania Museum and School for Industrial Arts, the collection had outgrown Memorial Hall by the turn of the century. By 1907, Fairmount was targeted for a new museum. Eli Kirk Price, Jr., directed the construction and was named the museum's president in 1926.

Left of the Washington Monument is ***Mounted Amazon Attacked by a Panther*** by Auguste Kiss and ***The Lion Fighter*** by Albert Wolff is on the right. The originals are at the National Museum of Berlin and both were installed here in 1929.

Prometheus Strangling the Vulture by Jacques Lipchitz, stands in front of the museum entrance. Prometheus stole fire from the gods and gave it to mankind. As punishment, he was chained to a rock and a vulture pecked at him incessantly. Here he has broken free and is strangling his tormentor. Lipchitz was a Lithuanian Jew who moved to Paris and became a noted sculptor in the Cubist movement. He and his wife fled from Paris to New York City in 1939.

Now continue around the museum back to the statue of John Marshall. Just before you exit the museum road, look at the two standing figures across the road. These are **Major General Peter Muhlenberg** by J. Otto Schweig, which was unveiled in 1910, and **Stephen Girard** by John Massey Rhind, which was unveiled in 1897. A biography of philanthropist and financier Girard is included with the description of Girard College in Tour 3.

Muhlenberg was the son of prominent Lutheran minister Henry Melchior Muhlenberg and served as a Lutheran minister in Virginia before joining the Continental Army during the American Revolution. Muhlenberg retired in 1783 and returned to Pennsylvania, where he served in several public offices, including congressman and senator.

9.9   Turn right and return to Twenty-fifth Street.

A gilded **Joan of Arc,** or "Joanie on a Pony" as she is affectionately known, banner held high, greets you on the other side of Kelly Drive at Twenty-fifth Street. The French government commissioned

Emmanuel Frémiet to create a monument to Joan of Arc for the Place des Pyramides in Paris. The Fairmount Art Association purchased a casting with the stipulation that only three would be made. In addition to this one and the one in Paris, the third is in Nancy, France. At one point, the artist performed a sleight of hand that resulted in Philadelphia receiving the original Joan; a second, slightly different version is in Paris. After at first installing the original cast in Paris, Frémiet made some small "improvements." He requested permission to remove the original and replace it with the new version, but the French government refused. When the art association made its offer, Frémiet saw his opportunity. He convinced the French that the statue would look much better gilded and asked to remove it to his studio to do the work himself. There, he gilded the other, newer version and returned that to the Place des Pyramides, shipping the older, ungilded one to Philadelphia. The deception was not noted for many years. In the meantime, Philadelphia had this Joan gilded as well.

9.95 Left onto the Kelly Drive bike path.

10.15 Left on Aquarium Drive.

10.25 End at the **Seahorses Fountain.**

Don't miss the chance to stroll through the **Azalea Garden** while you are here. It was originally planted in English Romantic style by the Pennsylvania Horticultural Society in 1952 on four acres of land. The azaleas are usually in bloom starting in early May and continuing through most of June. Other blossoms take over then, though none as profuse as the azaleas. Just past the arbor is the serene bronze *Puma,* created by Eric Berg in 1983.

Also, take a moment to see the **William M. Reilly Memorial,** installed between 1938 and 1960. This is the group of six statues of heroes of the American Revolution set between the Seahorses Fountain and the museum.

William Reilly, who died in 1890, was a general in the Pennsylvania National Guard. His will established a trust fund for a memorial to Revolutionary War heroes. In 1938, there were enough funds to com-

where the name changes to Lansdowne Drive. Next right in 0.3 mile, where Lansdowne Drive turns right. (The road straight ahead becomes South Concourse Drive.) Straight in 0.1 mile through the Civil War Memorial Arch. Memorial Hall is on the right in 0.3 mile.

SERVICES: Small restaurants and delis on Ford Road and Conshohocken Avenue (mile 3.1). West River Drive is closed to motorized traffic on weekends from April to October.

BIKE SHOPS: Wolff Cycle, 4311 Lancaster Ave (215) 222-2171 (not on route), and **Drive Sports,** 2601 Pennsylvania Ave (215) 232-7368 (not on route).

In 1869, private citizens purchased the Lansdowne estate on the west bank of the Schuylkill River. They then sold the land to the city of Philadelphia for the same price they paid, to be included in Fairmount Park, the great public park begun on the river's east bank a few years earlier.

The west park received a significant boost in popularity with the 1876 Centennial Exposition of the United States, a national extravaganza that showed off Philadelphia's love of public art and its achievements in technology. Memorial Hall was the only permanent structure built by the city for the exposition. After the centennial closed, it became the city's primary art museum until 1928, when the Philadelphia Museum of Art opened in East Fairmount Park. Today, several city agencies have offices in Memorial Hall.

You will ride through the grounds of the Fairmount Horticultural Center. You can stop for an extended walk through formal gardens or a more natural wooded setting. You will also see the Japanese House, Shofu-So, or Pine Breeze Villa. Next you will climb up to Belmont Plateau and be rewarded with an excellent view of the city skyline from Belmont Mansion, before wooded park roads take you down a bike path for a flat ride along the west bank of the river. On your way back to Memorial Hall, you will pass the Philadelphia Zoo and the Letitia Street House, one of the oldest buildings in the city.

0.0   Begin at Memorial Hall, going west on North Concourse Drive.

Philadelphia was the country's wealthiest and largest city at the time of the American Revolution. But when the nation's capital moved to Washington, D.C., in 1800, and New York City became the new banking center during the first half of the nineteenth century, the city went into decline. It took the Industrial Revolution to begin Philadelphia's resurgence as a city of importance. Factories sprang up around the city, and during the Civil War, businesses provided uniforms, arms, ammunition, and other supplies for the Union Army. The resulting economic boost continued into the next decade.

As memories of the bloody Civil War began to fade, Americans were eager for reasons to celebrate as the country's Centennial approached. The decision to host a national celebration in Philadelphia pushed the city into a new period of prosperity, civic pride, and dedication to public art.

The Centennial Exposition took ten years to plan and cost more than $11 million. There were more than two hundred buildings on the 450 acres in West Fairmount Park. The exposition was essentially a trade fair, the first of its kind in the United States. The buildings were designed in various architectural styles popular around the country at the time.

Opening ceremonies were on May 10, 1876, when President Ulysses S. Grant and Dom Pedro, emperor of Brazil, threw the two switches that started the huge Corliss duplex engine, the largest steam engine in the world. By the time the fair closed six months later, the city, with a population of under one million, hosted more than ten million people who came to view more than thirty thousand exhibitions.

Munich-born Herman J. Schwarzmann was chosen to design five buildings for the exposition, including **Memorial Hall**. He had never before designed a building and was sent to Vienna to study an 1873 exhibition to learn the art of architecture. Memorial Hall is in Beaux-Arts style with ornamental sculpture and terra-cotta on façades and at the roofline. It was the model for several other museums in the country including the Metropolitan Museum of Art in New York City. It also influenced the design of the Reichstag, the German parliament

MEMORIAL HALL IN WEST FAIRMOUNT PARK

building in Berlin, and is credited as the first American building to influence European architecture.

The glass and iron dome rises 150 feet above the ground with the figure of **Columbia** perched on the top. As large as the current sculpture is, it's hard to believe that the original statue, which was damaged in a thunderstorm and replaced in 1901, was considerably larger. The dome was originally lit with gas lamps; the current lighting is meant to re-create that effect.

A. M. J. Mueller sculpted *Columbia* and the statues at the corners of the roof, *Art, Science, Industry, Commerce, Agriculture,* and *Mining,* around 1876. The statues of **Pegasus** by Vincent Bildhauer Pilz in front of Memorial Hall were designed for the Imperial Opera House in Vienna in 1861. The Austrian emperor felt they were too big for that building, and they ended up with the Fairmount Park Commission.

Memorial Hall was originally called the Centennial Art Gallery and was the first home of what is now the Philadelphia Museum of Art. In 1873, the state legislature chartered the Pennsylvania Museum and School of Industrial Arts with an emphasis on development of the textile industries, intending for it to reside in Memorial Hall. The art collection outgrew the buildings even before the exposition opened, and a brick annex was added. The school was planned for another location but continued to outgrow homes for fifteen years until it was finally relocated to Broad and Pine Streets, where it continues today as the University of Arts (Tour 4). The art museum moved to East Fairmount Park in 1928, but Memorial Hall remained an art museum until 1954, when it was converted to offices for various city agencies, including the Fairmount Park Commission. A recently restored forty-foot model of the Centennial Exposition grounds is currently in the basement.

The Centennial Exposition was the largest public art collection in the United States, incorporating the most popular styles found in Europe. Some of the art generated much controversy, especially the Women's Pavilion, which displayed the artwork of fifteen hundred women from thirteen countries. At the time, the role of women in society was changing radically. The National Women's Suffrage Association presented "A Declaration of Rights for Women," read by Susan B. Anthony, at Independence Hall in 1876. And yet it was still considered scandalous for women to create, pose for, or even look at some forms of art, especially nudes. Not all of the women's art was controversial, however; a favorite piece was *The Dreaming Iolanthe (A Study in Butter)* by Caroline S. Brooks. This ethereal relief was sculpted entirely out of butter and displayed in a cooled tin frame.

In 1876, Frédéric-Auguste Bartholdi was working on the Statue of Liberty, and a Centennial Exposition commissioner arranged to ship the arm holding the torch to Philadelphia for display. It was forty-two-feet high with an eight-foot forefinger. Visitors could enter the arm and climb up to an observation deck at the base of the torch.

Facing Memorial Hall, turn left and ride along the street in front of the building toward Belmont Avenue.

0.25 Right on Belmont Avenue.

There is a multi-use path parallel to Belmont Avenue and you may want to use it, although it is in need of repair. This street has no shoulder and traffic can be heavy and fast.

0.6 Right at the "No Outlet" sign before you reach the traffic light. Go around the barriers and continue toward the gates and fountain at the entrance to the Horticultural Society grounds.

0.75 Follow the road straight through the gates of the grounds of the **Fairmount Park Horticultural Center** (summer, daily 9–6; winter, daily 9–5).

There is a map of the grounds on a sign just inside the gates on the right. If you have the time, consider walking your bike along some of the paths. There are reflecting pools, gazebos, and arches that are surrounded by an ever-changing display of plants and flowers.

1.0 The **Horticultural Center** is on the right.

1.05 Left after the parking area.

The statue of the dignified gent at the back is **Reverend Doctor John Witherspoon,** an exhibit for the Centennial provided by the Presbyterian Church in Philadelphia. There are also busts of several classical music composers, including **Schubert** and **Verdi.** The fountain at the rear was moved from Twelfth and Spring Garden Streets where it was originally installed in 1908 by the Fountain Society. It was widely recognized that plentiful, clean water was essential to good health, but it was not always readily available, especially to poor city dwellers. Several charitable societies emerged during the nineteenth century to provide water through the construction of public fountains. This sculpture was part of one of those projects. It was moved to this location in 1934.

1.1 Left on the main road.

Another garden is on the right just past the Horticultural Society Center. You can see the back of the sculpture *Night* by Edward Stauch. This was the first work of art held by the Fairmount Park Art Association.

Edwin N. Benson, a founding member of the Art Association, purchased it in 1872.

There are more extensive gardens that include a stone Japanese lantern, several benches, and the impressive Pavilion in the Trees to the left. To the right, you can see a 1903 **sundial** by Alexander Stirling Calder, the middle generation of Philadelphia's most famous family of artists (Tour 3). A little farther are steel sculptures of horses, *Gambol I* and *Gambol II,* by Robert David Lasus, placed here in 1992. You will need to walk your bike on all of these paths.

1.3   Left to go around the **Japanese House**.

Continue around the enclosure by bearing right. As you travel around, be sure to look through the fence at the beautiful pond and garden.

The Japanese House, Shofu-So, or Pine Breeze Villa (May–Oct., Tu–F 10–4, Sa–Su 12–6) is a reconstruction of a seventeenth-century Japanese scholar's house, teahouse, and garden and was designed in 1953 by Junzo Yoshimura. It was first displayed at the Museum of Modern Art in New York City and was refurbished by the Japanese government for the American Bicentennial in 1976.

1.35 Continue around the Japanese House and go back toward the Horticultural Center.

The Journeyer by Lindsay Daen is on the right just before the Horticultural Center.

1.8   Go out through the gates and turn right.

1.9   Straight across Montgomery Drive and continue on Belmont Mansion Drive.

This is your biggest challenge. Go up the hill to **Belmont Mansion**, past ball fields on the right. You will get your reward after about 0.25 mile when you look to the right at a fine view of the city skyline.

Belmont Mansion, about 240 feet above the Schuylkill River, was built on land purchased by Judge William Peters in 1742. Peters was a Loyalist and returned to England as the Revolutionary War loomed. His son, Richard, was a Patriot and entertained many influential colo-

THE JOURNEYER BY LINDSAY DAEN, GROUNDS OF THE PENNSYLVANIA HORTICULTURAL SOCIETY

CITY SKYLINE FROM BELMONT PLATEAU IN WEST FAIRMOUNT PARK

nial Americans, including George Washington, Benjamin Franklin, and James Madison. The house has changed appearances and, of course, owners through the years. The oldest section of the house may date to 1755, and the newest section was constructed around 1844.

2.5 Right at the stop sign on Chamounix Drive.

There is a hostel at the end of this road in Chamounix Mansion, one of the park's historic houses. The Chamounix Stables are also nearby, offering programs for city kids to learn to ride horses.

3.1 Left at the bottom of the hill on Ford Road.

Go under the stone bridge and head back up hill. You are leaving Fairmount Park.

3.4 Right at the first traffic light on Cranston Road.

3.5 Follow Cranston Road to the left where Dauphin Road joins from the right.

3.6 Right on Conshohocken State Road at the traffic light. There are a couple of sharp turns on this road, so stay alert.

In about 0.5 mile you will reenter the park and onto a bike lane. Keep following the winding road down hill to the river.

4.45 Right at the "T" at the stop sign onto Neill Drive (unmarked).

READ THESE INSTRUCTIONS BEFORE YOU CONTINUE. In 0.25 mile you will reach West River Drive. You will continue to ride on this side of the river. On weekends from April to October, West River Drive is closed to motorized traffic and you can ride straight ahead and ride on the road. At other times, ride on the bike path that runs between the drive and the river. When the drive is not closed to traffic, it is safest to cross the river on the sidewalk on the left side of the Falls Bridge. When you reach the other side, use the traffic light to cross the street and then double back across the bridge. Then you can safely join the bike path without jousting with cars.

4.7 Join West River Drive.

This is the **Falls Bridge,** a more permanent replacement for six previous bridges. The first was a chain suspension bridge, built in 1808 and destroyed by a heavy snowfall in 1816. It was replaced by a wire suspension bridge, the first in America and perhaps a prototype in need of study, as it lasted only six months before snow and ice destroyed it. Four wooden bridges also lost the battle with winter in 1822, 1850, 1878, and 1893. The current bridge was built using a modified truss that could withstand heavy loads. The designers must have had faith in it, because despite nearly a century of bridges being washed away by snow and ice, the original proposal called for a double-decker bridge. The top deck was intended for trolleys and trains coming from the bluffs on the east and west banks above the river, but it was never installed.

Before plumbing was readily available, streams running into the river were made more accessible by adding **stone and cement fountainheads.** You can see one of these on the right about 0.1 mile after the Falls Bridge. Most of the streams were smaller than this and were capped in the 1960s, although the fountainheads remain scattered along both banks of the river.

You will ride under **Strawberry Mansion Bridge** at 4.9 miles. This bridge was built in 1896–1897 by the Fairmount Park Transportation Company to carry trolleys and pedestrians from East to West Fairmount Park. At that time, the park was very popular but access was limited. The trolley traveled 8.8 miles from near Woodford Mansion in the East Park through the grounds of the West Park. The last trolley run was in 1946.

Boelston Cottage is on the right at 6.0 miles. The Fairmount Park Commission uses this house for many of its operations.

The large **barn** a little farther on the right houses the Belmont Stables, home of Philadelphia police horses.

Ride under the **Columbia Bridge** at 6.3 miles. The first bridge in this location was built in 1834 to help Pennsylvania businesses compete with the newly opened Erie Canal. The canal made it easier to transport goods to and from the rapidly developing western states by completing a waterway from New York City to Lake Superior. In response, Pennsylvania built seven hundred miles of railroads and canals from Philadelphia to Pittsburgh. The canal boats were designed to fit onto special flatbed railroad cars. The Main Line began operation in 1834 by traveling over the river on a covered wooden bridge. On this side, the cars were pulled up a ramp by rope all the way to the top of Belmont Plateau. When more strength was needed to carry increasingly heavy loads, a new bridge was built in 1886. This was replaced by the current bridge in 1920.

The statue of **St. George and the Dragon,** on the left at 6.5 miles, was once on top of the headquarters for the Society of the Sons of St. George, described as an organization "dedicated to helping English people in distress in America." The society moved out of the city in 1901 and the building was demolished.

Next to St. George is **Alexander von Humboldt** by Johann Heinrich, donated by "German citizens of Philadelphia to commemorate the Centenary of the Republic."

Humboldt, a German who lived from 1769 to 1859, was a passionate botanist and geologist who lobbied the Spanish government to explore Central and South America. From 1799 to 1804, Humboldt and a companion traveled more than six thousand miles on horseback, by canoe, and on foot. Data he published from his expeditions vastly increased the field of geology and formed the foundations of the modern studies of climatology and ecology. He spent much of the last twenty-five years of his life writing *Kosmos,* one of the greatest scientific textbooks ever written.

7.35 Right at the traffic light at Sweetbriar Drive.

7.4 Left at the stop sign onto Lansdowne Drive.

The **Philadelphia Zoo** (daily 9:30–5) is straight ahead at the traffic light at Girard Avenue in 0.2 mile. The oldest in the country, the zoo was chartered in 1859 as the Zoological Society of Philadelphia. The Civil War was already rumbling, however, and it was 1874 before the zoo opened with more than two thousand animals on display. Thousands of people waited in line on opening day.

Throughout the years, the zoo has been a leader in the births of endangered species in captivity, witnessing the first births in U.S. zoos of an orangutan, a chimpanzee, and a cheetah.

The news hasn't always been good, however. In 1995, the worst fire in American zoo history killed twenty-three endangered primates. Three years later, the PECO Primate Reserve opened with ten species, including western lowland gorillas, Sumatran orangutans, white-handed gibbons, and a variety of lemurs and monkeys. The reserve has been cleverly designed to resemble an abandoned timber mill.

Today, the zoo houses more than sixteen hundred animals representing four hundred species. You can see giraffes, zebra, sable antelopes, and secretary birds in the African plains section, and the reptile and amphibian house is one of the largest in the country. In the children's zoo, the first in the world, kids can get up close and personal with tamer species. You can also visit the Treehouse, a four-story replica of a tropical tree, for a Tarzan's eye view of the animal world. For a panoramic view of the city you might want to try the Zooballoon (daily 9:30–5, weather permitting), a tethered, helium-filled balloon that lifts passengers four hundred feet in the air.

7.6   Right on Girard Avenue.

7.7   Right into the driveway for the Letitia Street House.

The **Letitia Street House** is one of the oldest documented buildings in Philadelphia. Built in the early 1700s, it was moved here in 1833 from Letitia Street between Front and Second Streets. For a long time it was thought that William Penn purchased this house for his daughter, but in the twentieth century it was determined to have had nothing to do with the Penn family. The public tours were stopped and the house is now home of the Wildlife Preservation Trust International and the Nature Conservation Program.

7.8   Turn around and go back to Girard Avenue. You may find it easiest to walk back on the sidewalk if traffic on Girard Avenue is heavy.

7.9   Left on Lansdowne/Thirty-fourth Street. The street is Lansdowne to the left, but it becomes Thirty-fourth on the opposite side of Girard Avenue.

8.0   Straight through the stop sign to stay on Lansdowne Drive.

8.5   Next right where Lansdowne Drive turns right. The road straight ahead becomes South Concourse Drive.

8.6   Straight at the stop sign where Lansdowne Drive becomes North Concourse Drive.

8.7   Straight through the **Smith Civil War Memorial**.

Richard Smith, who earned a fortune through his invention of electroplate typesetting, bequeathed a half million dollars to Fairmount Park to construct a Civil War memorial. The figures atop the pedestals are Majors General John Fulton Reynolds and George Gordon Meade, by Charles Grafly and Daniel Chester French, respectively. Major General Winfield Scott Hancock by John Quincy Adams Ward and Major General George Brinton McClellan by Edward Clark Potter are on horseback at the outside of the arches. Among the seven Civil War heroes depicted in busts is James H. Windrim, who designed the memorial. Windrim also included a full-length sculpture of Richard Smith, which is the lowest standing figure on the right side. It took fifteen years, from 1897 to 1912, to finish the memorial, and it was finally unveiled without ceremony because interest in the Civil War had waned as another war of global proportions loomed.

Take a moment to stop behind the memorial and walk over to the benches located on either side of the curved walls. These are known as the **whispering benches,** and you can test them if you have a companion. Sit at opposite ends of the benches and whisper to each other. The curve of the wall conducts sound with amazing clarity and volume.

8.9   End at Memorial Hall.

SMITH MEMORIAL ARCH, WEST FAIRMOUNT PARK

ATTRACTIONS IN WEST FAIRMOUNT PARK

Philadelphia Zoo, 3400 West Girard Avenue (215) 243-1100, fax (215) 243-5385, daily 9:30–5, http://www.philadelphiazoo.org, admission.

Fairmount Park Horticultural Center Grounds: summer, daily 9–6; winter, daily 9–5, http://www.pennsylvaniahorticulturalsociety.org, free.

Japanese House, Horticultural Center Grounds (215) 685-0000,

May–Oct., Tu–F 10–4, Sa–Su 12–6, http://www.shofuso.org, admission.

Zooballoon, Philadelphia Zoo, Thirty-fourth Street and Girard Avenue (215) 243-5700, daily 9:30–5, weather permitting, http://www.channel6zooballoon.com, admission.

Germantown and East Mount Airy

DISTANCE: 8.5 miles, 14 km

TERRAIN: Moderately hilly. Paved roads with light traffic except three short sections on Germantown Avenue where I suggest you walk your bike.

START: Market Square, on the east side of Germantown Avenue and School House Lane.

ACCESS BY CAR: From I-76 take the Lincoln Drive exit. Follow signs to Lincoln Drive. Right at the first traffic light onto Rittenhouse Street. Right at the next traffic light onto Wissahickon Avenue. Left at the second traffic light onto School House Lane. Cross Germantown Avenue in five blocks and immediately turn right onto Market Square. Germantown Historical Society is on the left in this block, and there is parking on the street.

ACCESS BY PUBLIC TRANSPORTATION: Take **SEPTA Regional Rail Line R8, Chestnut Hill West** to Chelten Avenue. North on Chelten Avenue less than one block. Turn right on Pulaski Street. Left on School House Lane in one block. Cross Germantown Avenue in three blocks and immediately turn right onto Market Square. Germantown Historical Society is on the left on this block.

SERVICES: Restaurants just off of Germantown Avenue between Armat Street and School House Lane (near the start). Also, the Trolley Car Diner is two blocks from Gowen Avenue to the right on Germantown Avenue (a block from mile 4.35), Park Manor Deli is to the left

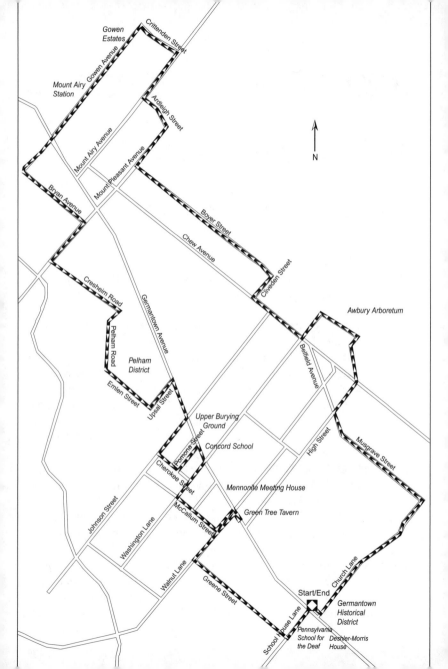

Gowen Estates

Crittenden Street

Gowen Avenue

Mount Airy Station

Mount Airy Avenue

Ardleigh Street

Mount Pleasant Avenue

Bryan Avenue

Boyer Street

Chew Avenue

Cliveden Street

Cresheim Road

Germantown Avenue

Awbury Arboretum

Pelham Road

Pelham District

Belfield Avenue

Emlen Street

Upsal Street

High Street

Musgrave Street

Upper Burying Ground

Pomona Street

Concord School

Cherokee Street

Mennonite Meeting House

Johnson Street

McCallum Street

Green Tree Tavern

Washington Lane

Walnut Lane

Greene Street

Church Lane

Start/End

Germantown Historical District

School House Lane

Pennsylvania School for the Deaf

Deshler-Morris House

N

on Chelten Avenue (a block from mile 8.1). Public restrooms at Germantown Historical Society (start) and Awbury Arboretum (mile 1.5).

BIKE SHOPS: Lambert Cycle Shop, 6616 Germantown Avenue (215) 848-8893 (two blocks to the left on Germantown Avenue at mile 6.0) and **Bike Addicts,** 5548 Ridge Avenue (215) 487-3006 (not on route).

The character of Germantown has changed radically over the three hundred years that have passed since it was founded by Quakers in 1683. Though none of the original houses remain, you will pass Wyck, the oldest building in Germantown, built by one of the earliest settlers. It was originally constructed in 1690 and has been modified many times. Germantown was a quiet, rural community when wealthy city residents began building large summer estates here in the mid-1700s. Construction of homes accelerated with the 1793 yellow fever epidemic, when thousands of city dwellers moved here for the summer until the disease abated. Among these transient residents was President George Washington, who rented the Deshler-Morris House, located near the start of the tour. The tour will also take you through the Tulpehocken district, which sprang up in the mid-1800s when train service was extended to the area. You will see the carefully planned community of Pelham as well as Gowen Estate, another early suburb. Germantown remained prosperous into the middle of the twentieth century, but automobiles and interstate highways facilitated movement farther from the city. At the same time, less prosperous minority groups began to move into Germantown. Fearful of continuing economic decline, White families fled over the next few decades, and many properties were abandoned or neglected. Germantown has always been a politically active neighborhood with strong community spirit, however, and today you can see the effects of twenty years of restoration and economic development in these neighborhoods.

During the eighteenth century, Germantown Avenue was known as the worst road in the American colonies. One story tells of a man who purchased land on both sides of the road and used a horse to get from one to the other because it was too difficult to walk. Today you might be tempted to say it's the worst road in Philadelphia for bicycles. Much of it is paved with Belgian blocks and lined with trolley tracks that are frequently in need of repair. This route travels back and forth across the avenue rather than along it, but there are still a few short blocks where you will want to walk your bike.

0.0   Start at Market Square on the east side of Germantown Avenue at Church Lane.

The **Civil War Soldiers' and Sailors' Monument** was sculpted by John Lachmier in 1883. This site was chosen for the memorial because it was the center of the British line in the Battle of Germantown in 1777. The **Germantown Historical Society** (Tu, Th 9–5, Su 1–5) is on the corner of Church Lane on the east side of Market Square. Since 1901 the historical society has been very active in the community; it sponsors lectures, meetings and tours and is an active partner with the African American Genealogy Group.

A group of German-speaking Quakers purchased land from William Penn in 1683 through Daniel Francis Pastorius. Pastorius was a devout man who wanted to come to the Pennsylvania colony to lead "a quiet, Godly life in a howling wilderness" far from "sinful" European cities. He purchased 5,700 acres about six miles away from the Delaware River along an Indian trail, at first called the Great Road, now called Germantown Avenue. Lots were long and thin and each abutted the Great Road, which remained the only road for many years.

The formal name for the Quaker religion is the Society of Friends; it arose from Puritan roots in England in the mid-1600s and quickly spread to continental Europe. Quakers, like other Puritans, were persecuted in Europe, and William Penn, a Quaker convert, assured all Quakers that they would find a safe haven in the Pennsylvania colony. The Quaker religion emphasizes the value of a quiet, contemplative life with few luxuries. This philosophy extends to architecture, and the early settlers built simple, functional homes out of a local stone called Wissahickon schist.

Around the middle of the eighteenth century, when wealthy Philadelphia residents began to purchase property in Germantown for summer houses, the first of these were German-speaking Quakers who erected modest houses to blend in well so their presence was not strongly felt.

As the community along the Delaware River became more congested, Germantown became a popular place to get away from it all, and the yellow fever epidemic dramatically increased that movement. Yellow fever is spread by a mosquito usually found in tropical areas. Earlier outbreaks affected American colonies as far north as Boston, but the epidemic in Philadelphia in 1793 was catastrophic. Early in the summer a slave rebellion in Santo Domingo (now the Dominican Republic) brought more than a thousand refugees to Philadelphia. They also brought yellow fever, which spread rapidly due to overcrowding and poor sanitation. Ten percent of the city's population died that summer. By August physicians issued statements urging everyone who was able to leave to do so quickly, and the government was temporarily disbanded. Half the population fled until the disease abated.

At the time, no one knew what caused the disease. It was noted that areas of higher elevation were relatively free of yellow fever. Thus Germantown, the highest settlement in the area, was the location of choice for those fleeing the epidemic, and every available space was rented, purchased, borrowed, or otherwise invaded that summer. President George Washington rented the **Deshler-Morris House** (W, F, Sa, Su 1–4) located across the street from Market Square. Plans were also made for Congress to meet a few blocks away at Germantown Academy.

Most of Philadelphia's residents returned to the city after the epidemic, but some purchased large tracts of land for summer estates in the following years, and Washington again rented the Deshler-Morris House the following summer.

It must have been satisfying for Washington to run the new nation from the Deshler-Morris House, since it had been the headquarters of General William Howe, who commanded the British troops and defeated Washington during the Battle of Germantown. The house was owned by members of the Morris family until the mid-1900s, when the National Park Service made it part of Independence National Historic Park.

Ride on Church Lane past the historical society.

0.3   After riding under the railroad bridge, go straight at the stop sign at Baynton Street. Quickly bear right and immediately back to the left to go around the island and continue up the hill, remaining on Church Lane.

0.65 Left on Musgrave Street.

1.1   Straight where Musgrave Street becomes Belfield Avenue.

1.2   Next right on High Street.

1.4   Left on Chew Avenue, then an immediate right into **Awbury Arboretum** (daily dawn to dusk).

1.45 Left at the fork and continue into the arboretum.

1.6   Make a U-turn in front of the **Francis Cope House**.

Awbury was the summer estate of the Cope family. Purchased in 1852 by Henry Cope, several homes were built on the estate between 1852 and 1920. The Francis Cope House, built in 1860 for Henry's son, is now the home of the Awbury Arboretum offices. The Cope family converted the estate into an arboretum for public use and for horticultural education. Awbury Arboretum has won awards and accolades for its successful program that teaches marketable horticulture and landscaping skills to youths and adults. There are also numerous programs for area children. In 2002, the arboretum received a grant to construct a "secret garden" within the arboretum, scheduled for completion in 2005.

1.65 Right onto a paved road leading to the Washington Lane train station. Do not continue all the way back to Chew Avenue.

1.75 Right into the train station parking lot.

FRANCIS COPE HOUSE IN AWBURY ARBORETUM

1.8 Left on Washington Lane.

1.9 Right on Chew Avenue.

2.2 Right on Cliveden Street.

2.25 Hard left on Boyer Street. Do not turn onto Belfield Avenue.

This is East Mount Airy. Northwest Philadelphia was not part of the city of Philadelphia until 1854. Before then, it was all part of the German Township and included the areas now known as Mount Airy and Chestnut Hill. The population of East Mount Airy changed from predominantly White to predominantly Black during the 1960s and 1970s. This section attracted middle-income, professional families and quickly became one of the most economically stable African-American neighborhoods in the city.

　　Boyer Street is a charming section of East Mount Airy. You will pass a variety of modern residences, including some interesting and unique **Craftsman bungalows** near Gorgas Lane in about 0.5 mile. These one-and-a-half-story homes were popular in the 1920s and 1930s. The name comes from the magazine *The Craftsman* that sold plans for building many different houses. The thin, brown bricks on the bungalows' façades give them a rich color and texture.

3.0   Right on Mount Pleasant Avenue.

3.15   Left on Ardleigh Street.

3.35   Right on Mount Airy Avenue.

3.55   Left on Crittenden Street.

3.75   Left on Gowen Avenue.

The next great change came to the German Township with the arrival of the railroad in the mid-1800s. As is still the case today, changes in transportation have profound effects on the way we live. The train allowed businessmen to move farther out of the city and still commute to work every day. Thus, Germantown became one of the country's first commuter suburbs.

This area was once part of the 130-acre **Gowen estate**, begun in 1792 by Joseph Miller. Miller's house is located on the grounds of the Lutheran Theological Seminary at Germantown Avenue and Allen's Lane. Miller's daughter, Mary, married wine importer James Gowen and the couple moved into her father's house in 1794. Gowen's fortune grew and in 1834 he purchased the estate next to his, then owned by William Allen, chief justice of the Pennsylvania Supreme Court. Gowen razed Allen's mansion, Mount Airy, and built a grand Italianate mansion, Magnolia Villa, which is now also part of the seminary. Most of its Victorian decoration and trim were removed during the 1950s.

Gowen died in 1872, and his heirs began to develop the estate and construct roads through the property. His son, Franklin Benjamin Gowen, was president of the Reading Railroad, and the family used his influence to bring the train line through the estate, although an economic depression delayed construction of houses for a decade. The first

HOUSE ON EAST GOWEN AVENUE AND ARDLEIGH STREET

one was built in 1883, and the next generation of the family built nearly two hundred homes here, mostly for upper-class families. In 2001 the area was declared one of the prettiest neighborhoods in the country by *Victorian Homes* magazine.

Franklin Benjamin Gowen was involved in the infamous Molly Maguire trials. Franklin headed the Reading Railroad's legal department in 1867 and was elected president of the railroad in 1870. Owning several mines and with coal as its principal cargo, the railroad suffered as the price of coal fell. Layoffs, wage cuts, and an increasing number of accidents fueled the actions of a group of dissident and violent coal miners known as the Molly Maguires. The state named Franklin Gowen as special prosecutor, and under intense emotional and political pressure, many men were arrested and ten were hanged as a result of what is still considered sparse and unreliable evidence.

Around 4.0 miles, you will ride an overpass above the train line.

Take a look at the **Mount Airy train station** on the right. Like many of
the original stations, this one was designed in 1882 by Frank Furness
(Tour 10). The Reading Railroad was in direct competition with the
Pennsylvania Railroad to attract suburbanites to its district (Tour 9)
and sought a bit of an edge by improving services. Elegant stations with
comfortable waiting areas provided one way to do this.

4.35 Cross Germantown Avenue and continue on **West Gowen
Avenue**.

These homes are not as opulent as those east of Germantown Avenue,
but they are charming and beautifully maintained. They were constructed in the early 1900s.

4.55 Left on Bryan Street.

4.9 Right on Mount Pleasant Avenue.

5.1 Left on Cresheim Road.

This is another late 1800s garden suburb called the **Pelham District**.
This area, called Phil-Ellena, was the estate of George W. Carpenter
and named for his wife, Ellena. After his death, Carpenter's heirs began
the now-familiar process of dividing the estate. Significant care and
planning went into this development. The Carpenter Land and Developments Company was directed by Anthony J. Drexel (Tour 10) and
Edward J. Stotesbury, who hired a team of architects to draw up harmonious designs for upper-echelon families.

At the time, there were no zoning laws. However, the developers
imposed regulations that are now routinely used by zoning boards,
such as setback limits and restrictions on commercial property. The
result is a beautiful neighborhood with now-mature trees, wide streets,
and spacious yards and gardens.

Barnhurst is on the right at 6818 Cresheim Road just after Carpenter Lane. It was built on the foundations of the Carpenter estate's barn.
Nothing else remains of the original buildings. Barnhurst is now the
home of the **Cecilian Academy Convent**.

5.5   Right on **Pelham Road**.

There are several beautiful homes along both sides of Pelham Road.

On the opposite corner of this intersection you can see a Tudor-style home at **30 Pelham Road** designed by G. W. and W. D. Hewitt, who built many homes for Henry Houston in Chestnut Hill (Tour 9).

Straight across the intersection at **100 Pelham Road** is an elaborately decorated house with impressive limestone carvings.

Numbers 141 and **209** were designed by Horace Trumbauer, who also designed the Philadelphia Museum of Art.

During the 1970s and 1980s, many of the larger houses were converted for institutional use. Finding new uses for old buildings is often necessary; however, this can radically change the character of the neighborhood if too many family dwellings become commercial or institutional. This has become an increasingly important issue for neighborhoods in northwest Philadelphia and zoning disputes are common. Germantown and Mount Airy residents, known for liberal attitudes in politics and social issues, frequently must struggle with the balance between providing important services and maintaining the residential nature of a neighborhood.

5.7   Bear right on Phil-Ellena Street.

5.75 Quick left on Emlen Street.

6.0   Left on Upsal Street.

6.15 Right on Germantown Avenue. You may want to walk your bike this one block to Johnson Street.

Upsala (Th, Sa 1–4) is the Federal-style mansion on the right at 6430 Germantown Avenue. The original section of the house is at the rear and was built by John Johnson, Sr., father of the first resident of the Johnson House, which you will see in a few blocks. The front section of the home was built by the next Johnson generation in Federal style. The Johnson family owned this property until 1941.

Across the street at 6401 is **Cliveden** (Th–Su 12–4), built in 1763 by

Benjamin Chew, one of the city's most influential lawyers. Upsala is in the later Federal style, but Cliveden is mostly Georgian with typical Germantown elements to keep it simple enough for Chew's fellow Quakers.

Chew was a Tory and allowed British soldiers to take refuge here during the Battle of Germantown in 1777. This gave the British soldiers a strong advantage and they were able to repel the Continental Army, leading ultimately to the British takeover of the entire city. Chew paid for his loyalties after the war, when he and his family were briefly banished to the hinterland of New Jersey. He later repurchased the house, and it remained in the Chew family until 1972.

Cliveden sponsors special programs and field trips for children and adults, but it is best known as the site of the Battle of Germantown, which is reenacted here on the first Saturday in October each year. With arts and crafts and various activities in addition to reenactors in authentic costumes, it's a lot of fun.

6.3   Right on Johnson Street.

6.5   Left on Cherokee Street.

6.65   Left on Pomona Street.

6.75   Right on Germantown Avenue. Again, you may want to walk your bike for one block.

On the left you can see the **Upper Burying Ground** (Th–F 10–4, Sa 1–4), and **Concord Schoolhouse** (Th–F 10–4, Sa 1–4) at 6313 Germantown Avenue. The Upper Burying Ground was established in 1692 and contains the graves of soldiers of the Revolutionary War, the War of 1812, and the Civil War. Concord School was formed in 1775, when the Germantown Academy could no longer accommodate all the English-speaking children in Germantown.

The **Johnson House** (Th–F 10–4, Sa 1–4), on the right at 6306 Germantown Avenue, was built in 1768, for John Johnson, Jr., grandson of a Dutch immigrant. The Johnson family owned it until 1917, when it was purchased by the Women's Club of Germantown. They used it as their headquarters until the 1980s, when they gave it to the Mennonite Historic Trust as a house museum.

During the first half of the nineteenth century, Samuel Johnson allowed the house to be used as a stop on the Underground Railroad, the dangerous and arduous route taken by slaves escaping the South before the Civil War. Today, the Johnson House is the only accessible and intact Underground Railroad site in Philadelphia and is visited by many schools and tour groups, especially those interested in African-American history.

6.86 Right on Washington Lane.

Train service came to the Tulpehocken area in the 1840s, and houses were quickly built for the new commuters. Most of the homes were built on speculation and sold quickly after construction was complete. There were no rules to assure uniformity, so you will see a great variety of high Victorian architecture along these streets.

7.1 Left on McCallum Street.

7.25 Left on Walnut Lane.

7.35 Right on Germantown Avenue. Walk your bike for a half block.

The **Mennonite Meeting House** (open by appointment) is across Germantown Avenue on the left side of Walnut Lane at 6121. It was built in 1770 on the site of a log cabin that was the meeting house of the Mennonites who arrived here in 1683, the first in the New World.

Wyck (Apr.–Dec., Tu, Th, Sa 1–4) is to the right on this side of Germantown Avenue at 6026. Wyck is the oldest building in Germantown, although it has been altered over the years. Dutch Quaker Hans Milan erected the first building in 1690 out of Wissahickon schist. Family tradition states that Milan built a second home next to the first for his daughter. By the time of the American Revolution, the two houses were joined on the second floor with a carriageway underneath. In 1824, the family hired Greek Revival architect William Strickland to renovate the house. Where the carriageway had been, he added a new invention,

WYCK, GERMANTOWN AVENUE AND JOHNSON STREET

sliding glass doors, giving the residents a wonderful view of the rose garden. Nine generations of Milan's descendants lived in Wyck.

Today, the garden has been replanted, with cuttings from the original roses, in the same design as in the 1820s. The garden is nationally renowned and definitely worth a stop, especially when the roses are in bloom.

Green Tree Tavern is in the middle of the block opposite Wyck at 6023 Germantown Avenue. It was built in 1748 by the grandson of Germantown's founder, Daniel Francis Pastorius. Today it is the office of the First United Methodist Church of Germantown. When Green Tree Tavern was built, taverns were more than places to while away the time with a beer and a friend. They were the principal meeting places for conducting business, holding community meetings, and gathering the latest news.

7.4   Turn around and go back to Walnut Lane.

7.45   Left on Walnut Lane.

7.75   Left on Greene Street.

Vernon Park is on the left in 0.3 mile and is the location of **Center in the Park,** a community facility for seniors that is acclaimed for its educational programs and outreach services for house-bound individuals. The building was constructed in 1906 and renovated in the 1980s, winning awards from the American Institute of Architecture and the Foundation for Architecture.

8.25   Left on School House Lane.

The **Pennsylvania School for the Deaf** is at this intersection. This was the site of the Germantown Union School, established in 1761. You can see the original schoolhouse with two tiny buildings on either side. These were the quarters for the two schoolmasters, one for the German-speaking and one for the English-speaking students. At the time, Germantown was in transition from a rural German-speaking Quaker community to a haven for wealthy Philadelphia residents, most of whom spoke English. By 1810, English was dominant and classes were only held in English.

   The Pennsylvania School for the Deaf has obtained several buildings in the area, converting houses into classrooms and offices with little exterior change, maintaining the residential feel of the neighborhood.

8.35   Straight across Germantown Avenue.

8.4   Right on Market Square.

8.45   End at the Germantown Historical Society.

ATTRACTIONS IN GERMANTOWN

Awbury Arboretum, 1 Awbury Park (215) 849-2855, daily dawn to dusk, http://www.awbury.org, free.

Cliveden, 6401 Germantown Avenue (215) 848-1777, fax (215) 438-2892, Th–Su 12–4, http://www.cliveden.org, admission.

Concord School, 6309 Germantown Avenue (215) 843-0943, Th–F 10–4, Sa 1–4, admission.

Deshler-Morris House, 5442 Germantown Avenue (215) 596-1748, W, F, Sa, Su 1-4, http://www.nps.gov/demo/index.htm, Admission.

Germantown Historical Society, 5501 Germantown Avenue (215) 844-0514, fax (215) 844-2831, Tu, Th 9–5, Su 1–5, http://www.libertynet.org/ghs, admission.

Johnson House, 6306 Germantown Avenue (215) 843-0943, Th–F 10–4, Sa 1–4, admission.

Mennonite Meeting House, 6119 Germantown Avenue (215) 843-0943, open by appointment, admission.

Upper Burying Ground, 6311 Germantown Avenue (215) 843-0943, Th–F 10–4, Sa 1–4, included with admission to Concord School.

Upsala, 6430 Germantown Avenue (215) 842-1798, Th, Sa 1–4, http://www.cliveden.org/pages/upsala.htm, admission.

Wyck, 6026 Germantown Avenue (215) 848-1690, fax (215) 848-1612, Apr.–Dec., Tu, Th, Sa 1–4, http://www.wyck.org, admission.

The Wissahickon Gorge and West Mount Airy

DISTANCE: 8 miles, 13 km

TERRAIN: The first half is on a wide gravel road closed to motorized traffic and is flat. The second half is on paved roads with light traffic and has several short hills. There is a short section where you will need to walk your bike when you leave RittenhouseTown.

START: Valley Green Inn at the end of Wises Mill Road on Forbidden Drive.

ACCESS BY CAR: From I-76 take the Belmont Avenue exit. From eastbound I-76, turn left. From westbound I-76, turn right. Cross the river and continue up the hill where the name of the street becomes Green Lane. Turn left on Ridge Avenue in 0.9 mile. Turn right in one block on Dupont Avenue. At the "T" in 0.35 mile, turn left onto Henry Avenue. Turn right on Wises Mill Road in 1.6 miles. Continue to the bottom of the hill and bear right at 0.7 mile and park in the parking area for Fairmount Park and Valley Green Inn. You will ride southeast along Forbidden Drive past Valley Green Inn.

ACCESS BY PUBLIC TRANSPORTATION: Take **SEPTA Regional Rail Line R8 Chestnut Hill West** to St. Martin's Station. With your back to the station, turn left and go to Springfield Avenue. Turn right on Springfield Avenue for 0.4 mile. Immediately after passing Chestnut Hill Academy (on your right), bear right on Valley Green Road. Continue down the hill and cross the creek on the footbridge. Turn left onto Forbidden Drive after 0.7 mile and ride southeast to Valley Green Inn.

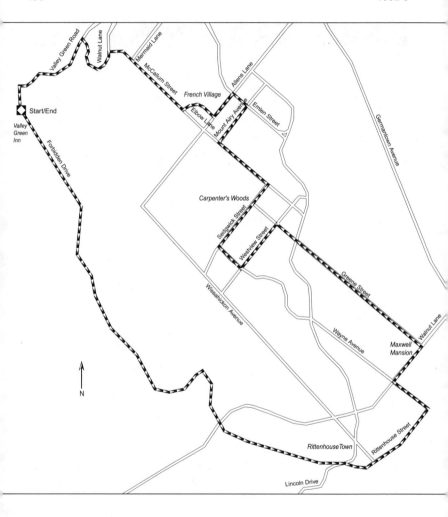

Valley Green Road

Walnut Lane

Mermaid Lane

McCallum Street

Alliens Lane

French Village

Start/End

Valley
Green
Inn

Forbidden Drive

Elbow Lane

Mount Airy Avenue

Emlen Street

Germantown Avenue

Carpenter's Woods

Sedgwick Street

Westview Street

Greene Street

Wissahickon Avenue

Wayne Avenue

Maxwell
Mansion

Walnut Lane

N

Rittenhouse Town

Rittenhouse Street

Lincoln Drive

SERVICES: Restaurant, snacks, and public restrooms at Valley Green at the start of the ride. There are no other places to buy food and drinks on the route.

BIKE SHOPS: Bike Addicts, 5548 Ridge Avenue (215) 487-3006 (not on route) and **Liberty Bell Bicycle Shop,** 6153 Ridge Avenue (215) 487-1850 (not on route).

In spite of the rise and fall of dozens of mills over the centuries, the Wissahickon Creek probably appears nearly as wild today as it did to the Lenni Lenape Indians who were the first people to visit here. It is hard to believe you are in the middle of Philadelphia when you ride along Forbidden Drive. The route takes you along the lower half of the drive from Valley Green Inn to RittenhouseTown. From there you will ride through the neighborhood of West Mount Airy.

"This Car Climbed Mount Airy" is one of my favorite Philadelphia bumper stickers. Mount Airy was the vastly overstated name of an eighteenth-century country estate. While you won't climb any mountains, you will need to climb a few hills. The area became the summer residence of wealthy Philadelphians in the early nineteenth century. Today, some of those early homes are still here, but mostly you will see more recent homes. One of Philadelphia's most charming neighborhoods, Mount Airy boasts meticulously maintained homes and bright, colorful front gardens among the early twentieth-century row houses and small twins. There are a number of mansions as well, but the more modest neighborhoods feel cozy and inviting. The area today is also known for its social activism and tightly knit community.

0.00 Start at **Valley Green Inn** (M–F 12–4, 5–9, Sa 10–4, 5–10, Su 10–3, 4–9).

Lenni Lenape Indians came to the Wissahickon Valley to hunt and fish long before Europeans discovered the area in the late seventeenth century. The name Wissahickon is believed to derive from the Lenni

**FEDERAL REVIVAL
DOORWAY, GREENE AND
RITTENHOUSE STREETS**

Lenape word for catfish or yellow-colored stream, "wisamickan" or "wissauchsikan," respectively.

The Lenape were part of the Algonquin Confederation. Although they could be found as far away as Long Island, most lived in the lower Delaware River Valley, and the first Europeans called them Delaware Indians. They were primarily farmers but their diet was heavily supplemented by fishing and hunting.

William Penn and his first advisors worked with the Lenni Lenape to reach an agreement that was mutually satisfactory. In exchange for payment in goods, Penn purchased a tract of land for the new immigrants. Penn returned to England permanently in 1701. In 1737, his sons and their representatives decided the original agreement was inadequate, and they devised the Walking Purchase, a hoax to convince the Lenapes to give up more land. The Penn sons drew up a phony document and told the Lenape that their ancestors had signed an agreement with William Penn's ancestors calling for the Indians to give up as much land as could be walked in a day and a half. The Lenape believed that sons are bound by the promises of their fathers and felt obliged to cooperate. Rather than allow the Lenape to accompany them on a casual walk from Philadelphia along the river on established trails, Penn's sons employed professional messengers to run the longest distance, stopping only for brief rests. Only one man lasted for a day and a half, but he covered more than fifty-eight miles. They knew they had been cheated, but the Lenape felt compelled to accept the new boundaries.

Like the other Indians of the northeast coast, the Lenni Lenape continued to be pushed west over the next 130 years until most ended up on a reservation in Oklahoma. A small group fled to Canada in 1890 and their ancestors live on two small reservations in Ontario. Today there are around three thousand members of the Lenape Nation.

The rock that makes up the gorge is known as **Wissahickon schist.** It is plentiful and easy to cut, making it a popular building material in colonial Philadelphia. There is mica, feldspar, and quartz in the schist, giving it a characteristic glitter. Most of the houses built in Germantown during the eighteenth century were made of Wissahickon schist. Visitors traveling on Germantown Avenue at that time commented on how the homes sparkled on sunny days.

One of the first Europeans to come to Wissahickon Creek was Johannes Kelpius, who arrived in 1694 with forty German followers. Kelpius was born Johann Kelp in 1673. He was a brilliant student and became a follower of Johann Jakob Zimmerman, a Pietist and mathematician who calculated that the Second Coming of Christ would occur in 1694. According to Zimmerman's interpretation of the Book of Revelation, Christ would return as a woman somewhere in the woods in the American colonies. His followers called themselves the "Contented of the God-Loving Soul," but were called the "Society of the Woman of the Wilderness" by outsiders. Zimmerman died in 1693 before the group left Germany, and Kelp, now using the Latinized name of Kelpius, was chosen to replace him as leader of the sect. Upon arrival in Philadelphia in early 1694, the group went to Germantown, the choice of most German immigrants at the time, where they built a large log cabin for community activities, with small single cells for sleeping and meditating. Kelpius lived alone in a cave that today is marked with a granite monolith. Hikers can reach the cave by following a trail off Hermit Lane, named for Kelpius.

The group remained mostly isolated from outsiders but did conduct public prayer services on Sundays, taught neighborhood children to read and write, and grew medicinal herbs, which they offered to anyone in need. Some followers left the group as time passed without the Second Coming, but most remained until Kelpius's death in 1708, when the commune disbanded.

During the nineteenth century the Wissahickon Gorge was attractive to artists and writers, who sang the praises of the unspoiled area. It became popular for recreational use and as an entertainment center, and several taverns were built on the banks of the creek. The taverns were fashionable sites for weddings and other gala events, and at least two of them featured live bears to entertain customers. Stories abound of people staggering from one tavern to another, or of horses that knew the route well enough that their riders could sleep it off between venues. Next to local ale, the most popular dishes were waffles and catfish.

By 1850, the Wissahickon Turnpike Company began to widen and improve the road that followed the creek all the way to the Schuylkill River. Fairmount Park obtained the upper half of the Wissahickon Valley in 1868, taking ownership of the road as well. From their first arrival, automobiles created controversy. They were banned in 1899, and although the issue was raised many times over the next decades, the "no motors" policy continued. Upper Wissahickon Drive then became known as Forbidden Drive. In addition to Forbidden Drive's 5.3-mile gravel road, there are more than forty miles of trails through the 1,800 acres owned by the park.

A drop of more than one hundred feet over seven miles made the creek an excellent site for mills. There were dozens here when Fairmount Park obtained the land as part of its attempt to prevent pollution of the city's drinking water in 1868 (Tour 5). By the mid-nineteenth century, waterpower was being supplanted by steam, and many of the mills had already been abandoned. The acquisition of the land was not only a great boon to city residents, it was also a bailout for the failing mill operators.

According to its universal policies, Fairmount Park banned alcohol, dooming the tavern business. Only two buildings remain: Valley Green Inn and the current headquarters of the 14th Police District on Lincoln Drive at Gypsy Lane, built in 1849.

You may still hear people say that Washington slept here, but George was long dead when **Valley Green Inn** was constructed in 1850. Today, the inn is owned by Fairmount Park but operated privately. They do have a liquor license, but I don't recommend trying to get your bike to drive you home while you snooze. The restaurant is expensive and quite good, but you can also get inexpensive snacks from a window on the side of the building. Reservations are highly recommended if you want to dine at the restaurant.

2.8   Left at the end of Forbidden Drive onto a smaller bike path.

Forbidden Drive ends at a parking area. Wissahickon Creek turns to the right here and Monoshone Creek joins it from the left.

At the end of Forbidden Drive on the left there is a plaque bolted to the rock that tells about the **Battle of Germantown** on October 4, 1777. The battle line extended for miles, starting here and ending on the other side of Germantown Avenue. Eleven thousand Continental troops fought against nine thousand British soldiers and Hessian mercenaries. The worst of the fighting was at Cliveden (Tour 7). The skirmish here was small and brief because of poor visibility in heavy fog. Although the Americans lost the battle, George Washington's innovative strategies and his win at Saratoga were credited with convincing the French to back the fledgling country's war of independence.

Just past the plaque, also on the left, you will see a small wooden building. This is the **Ten Box Shelter** constructed by the Works Project

BICYCLISTS ON FORBIDDEN DRIVE

Administration (WPA) in 1941. Established by the federal government as part of President Franklin Roosevelt's New Deal, it was a work program designed to help ease the country out of the Great Depression. WPA projects, scattered across the country, created jobs for 8.5 million people. Along Wissahickon Creek the WPA built a ten-box telephone network that ended here.

A bike path goes through the Ten Box Shelter to the left. Follow the path up the hill.

2.9   Left at the "T" and then immediately go right to follow a gravel road with Monoshone Creek on your right.

**RITTENHOUSETOWN,
LINCOLN DRIVE AND
RITTENHOUSE STREET**

This little cluster of buildings is **Historic RittenhouseTown**. The first paper mill in America was built here in 1690 by Wilhelm Rittenhausen, also the first Mennonite minister in the country. The Mennonites were followers of German Anabaptist Menno Simons. Persecuted in Europe, Mennonites came here in 1684, a year after German Quakers bought land in Germantown (Tour 7). Using the English spelling of his name, Rittenhouse came here from Holland in 1688. A devout and well-read follower of Simons, Rittenhouse was elected minister in 1690 and bishop in 1706, a year before his death.

Paper mills were rare even in England at the time, and this one was a source of great pride to William Penn. When a flood washed the first mill away in 1701, Penn helped finance the replacement. The mill and its owners prospered and other mills were built in the area. Succeeding generations of the family built homes here and sold property for other mill workers to build homes as well. In the mid-1800s there were more than forty buildings in RittenhouseTown, although only seven survive today. In addition to the six buildings visible on this road, there is a barn to the left, behind the cluster of houses. With an appointment, visitors can learn about papermaking and even try some techniques themselves.

All of the homes in RittenhouseTown are owned by Fairmount Park. Some are rented to families. Three of the four houses on this side of the creek were built by later generations of the Rittenhouse family. The first building you will pass is the sole nonfamily dwelling, and may be the oldest, built by Dutch or Swedish settlers about the time William arrived here. The other three houses are from the 1700s. The **visitor's center** (late Apr.–early Oct., Sa–Su 12–4) is the last building on the left. In 2002 the Philadelphia Committee of the Garden Club of America completed its revitalization project for the grounds surrounding the center.

3.1   Turn right to cross the creek on a wooden footbridge. You should walk your bike at this point.

The two buildings on the opposite side of the creek are part of William Rittenhouse's original homestead. The tiny house to the left contains a sixteen-foot fireplace, reportedly the largest in the colonies at the time. The section of the larger home that contains the chimney was built by Rittenhouse in about 1702 and was his home after the second mill was built.

The newer section of this larger house is the birthplace of David Rittenhouse, William's great-grandson and a prominent inventor and scientist. With little formal education, David learned mathematics and geometry from books, and he made models with a tool kit he inherited from an uncle who built furniture. David greatly advanced the science of making precision instruments, and he designed and built highly prized clocks and other instruments at a time when they were rare and in great demand. As good at using his instruments as he was at building them, Rittenhouse built the surveying instruments for and supervised the work on the Mason-Dixon Line, the most important surveying project at that time. After building the first telescope in this country, he was one of the first astronomers to view the atmosphere of Venus. Rittenhouse also introduced the use of spider's silk for the crosshairs of telescopes. A variety of other instruments came from Rittenhouse's workshop, including barometers, thermometers, and hygrometers. RittenhouseTown maintains a small herb garden behind the houses that is arranged as it might have been in the eighteenth century.

Walk past these two buildings on the footpath to the right of the white fence toward the major road in front of you. Just before you get to the road, turn left on the sidewalk and go to the traffic light. This is Lincoln Drive, so-named in the twentieth century, but built in 1826 along the original path that led from what is now RittenhouseTown to the Schuylkill River.

3.2 Cross Lincoln Drive in the pedestrian crosswalk and continue straight on Rittenhouse Street.

This is one of Philadelphia's cruel jokes on cyclists. Although you can get to this intersection legally and safely riding your bike on the bike path, once you get here you have to do a little shuffling around. You will be deposited on the sidewalk on the left side of Rittenhouse Street. When you judge it to be safe, cross the road and continue up the hill on Rittenhouse Street.

The triangular park on the left is **Saylor's Grove**. The Monoshone Creek ran through this park until the late 1900s, when it was diverted to give more usable park space. This diversion caused problems with the flow of water throughout this region, however, and there are now plans to remove it and allow the creek to return to its original path. The sculpture *Children at Play* by Peter Rockwell was placed here in 1978, before the creek was diverted, and will remain here.

3.0 Continue straight after the traffic light at Wissahickon Avenue.

3.6   Left on Wayne Avenue.

This is the **Tulpehocken Historic District**. The railroad was extended to
this area in 1832 and changed a sleepy rural community into a garden
suburb. Many houses were built on speculation and sold quickly when
property values increased. Plots of land were sold and developed indi-
vidually, unlike the planned community of the Pelham District (Tour
7). Pelham has some uniformity in architectural style, but the Tulpehocken district is a mix of several Victorian styles. The Victorians liked
exuberant displays of decorative detail, which was facilitated by the
invention of the jigsaw that allowed the highly carved "gingerbread"
details seen on porches and under eaves. Some of the larger buildings
have been transformed into apartment buildings. There is a growing
trend toward historic restoration, however, and some of them have
been converted back into single-family homes.

   At 3.7 miles, the **Charles Lister Townsend House** is at 6015 Wayne
Avenue, on the right after crossing Harvey Street. This house was built
in 1887 by G. W. and W. D. Hewitt, who also designed most of Henry
Howard Houston's houses in Chestnut Hill (Tour 9). Townsend was
the president of the Philadelphia stock exchange and used his wealth to
emulate Houston, erecting this grand twelve-bedroom castle as a
smaller version of Houston's home, Druim Moir.

3.9   Right on Walnut Lane.

4.1   Left on Greene Street.

Two of the grandest homes in the area are at this intersection, on the
right on either side of Greene Street. The **Mitchell mansion** is at 200
West Walnut Street, built in 1856, and **Gray Tower** is across Greene
Street, built around 1860.

   The gem of the neighborhood, however, is the **Ebenezer Maxwell
Mansion** on the corner of Greene and Tulpehocken Streets at 200 West
Tulpehocken Street (F–Su 1–4) on the left. Built in 1859, it was probably designed by Joseph C. Hoxie or Samuel Sloane, both popular architects of the Victorian age. Maxwell was a textile merchant who lived

here only a short time before selling the house for a nice profit as property values rose.

Drastic change in commuting patterns occurred again in the 1950s with the construction of interstate highways, which prompted another exodus out of the city. Along with developments built farther from Center City came a strong aversion to Victorian style, and grand houses like the Maxwell mansion were in jeopardy. In the 1950s, plans to build a gas station on this spot brought neighbors out to protest the intrusion of a commercial property, rather than to save the building itself. A second proposal in the 1960s was rejected, once again largely due to the efforts of a small group of tenacious neighbors. The mansion was converted to a house museum at that time, and it is still run mostly through the work of volunteers. The gardens behind Maxwell were designed in the style of A. J. Downing, a leading Victorian landscape architect. The mansion hosts several special events during the year, including an ice cream social in the summer, an open house in December, and popular ghost walks in October. For the latter, small groups are guided on a short tour of neighborhood, stopping at five or six places to hear original ghost stories written and told by members of Patchwork, a local storytellers guild.

4.9   Left on Westview Street.

This section of the route gives you a short tour of one of Mount Airy's prettiest neighborhoods. West Mount Airy has received national attention for its successful racial integration. Very few communities in America have achieved a stable mix of ethnic groups, and in Mount Airy it was created by design. In 1953, several religious organizations joined with community leaders to craft a statement titled "This We Believe About Our Neighborhood," a celebration of ethnic diversity whose aim was to prevent the sort of "white flight" that other parts of the city were experiencing. The following year, the group organized under the name West Mount Airy Neighbors and began sponsoring events to help new and old neighbors get to know one another. By the end of the decade, meetings drew hundreds of people who not only accepted the racial mix but were proud of their socially progressive neighborhood. West Mount Airy Neighbors continues to promote this tradition today, and ethnic diversity is one of the community's strongest assets.

The spirit of community extends beyond ethnicity. Weaver's Way Co-op (M–Th 10–8, F 9–8, Sa–Su 9–6), the Sedgwick Cultural Center, and the Arts League of Mount Airy (ALMA) (F 6–8, Sa–Su 1–5), all a few blocks from here, are successful cooperative enterprises that provide support to local groups. Established in 1973, Weaver's Way is a food store that also runs a recycling program and gives the profits to local organizations for community projects. The Sedgwick Cultural Center was established in 1992 and sponsors cultural and informal educational programs about music, arts and crafts, and dance for and by local residents. ALMA is run by volunteers and sponsors exhibits and programs to benefit and support local artists.

5.3   Right on Wayne Avenue.

5.5   Right on Sedgwick Street.

Carpenter's Woods, a little finger of Fairmount Park, is on the left. George W. Carpenter owned a huge estate in this area that extended from Wissahickon Avenue to Germantown Avenue.

5.85 Left on McCallum Street.

6.2   Right on West Mount Airy Avenue.

6.4   Left on Emlen Street.

6.5   Left on Allens Lane.

6.6   Right on Elbow Lane. Then follow the road as it bends to the left.

French Village, a small enclave of Gothic houses, was built by George Woodward, son-in-law of Henry Howard Houston. Houston owned three thousand acres in what is now Chestnut Hill and used his considerable influence to extend the railroad through his holdings (Tour 9). Upon Houston's death in 1895, Woodward took over development of the family property.

Both men exerted tight control over their holdings, but Woodward had more esthetic interest than his father-in-law did. He was fascinated by houses he saw on a trip to Normandy and decided that Philadelphia needed that kind of ambiance. While the houses are privately owned today, in Woodward's lifetime, they were rented.

While Houston was a businessman, Woodward was a visionary. Graduating from Yale and the University of Pennsylvania School of Medicine, he practiced medicine briefly but was more attracted to public health and used his position in society and his family wealth to improve the lot of Philadelphia's poor. He was a director of the Octavia Hill Association that worked to rehabilitate slums and rent them to the poor at low cost. He was also instrumental in creating a licensing and inspection division in the city in 1907 to assure that housing met certain health and safety standards. As a Pennsylvania state senator for more than thirty years, Woodward used that office to further his causes. He organized and financed the Child Labor Association of Pennsylvania and the Children's Aid Society. The former pressed for labor laws and the latter raised money to buy food, clothing, and medical supplies for poor children.

Woodward was also something of an eccentric: he always wore golf knickers and knee socks, even in Senate chambers. He used kerosene lamps to read and refused to drive cars with gas engines. He maintained two electric cars for decades, until his death in 1952.

6.8   Right on McCallum Street.

The Allens Lane Art Center, one of the oldest community-based cultural institutions in the country, is on the opposite side of McCallum, to the left. Sitting on six acres of land bequeathed by Gertrude Houston Woodward in 1928, the center has programs and facilities for adults and children in theater, dance, arts and crafts, and sports. The summer camp is particularly popular.

7.1   Straight to stay on McCallum Street where the main road turns right and becomes Mermaid Lane.

7.3   Left on Woolcott Drive at the "T."

7.5   Left on Valley Green Road at the "T."

7.9   End at Valley Green Inn.

ATTRACTIONS IN WEST MOUNT AIRY

Arts League of Mount Airy (ALMA), 7137 Germantown Avenue (215) 248-2573, F 6–8, Sa–Su 1–5, free.

Ebenezer Maxwell Mansion, 200 West Tulpehocken Street (215) 438-1861, F–Su 1–4, admission.

Historic RittenhouseTown, 206 Lincoln Drive (215) 438-5711, late Apr.–early Oct., Sa–Su 12–4, http://www.rittenhousetown.org, admission.

Sedgwick Cultural Center, 7137 Germantown Avenue (215) 248-9229, hours vary according to event schedule, http://www.sedgwickcenter .org, admission.

Valley Green Inn, Wises Mill Road and Forbidden Drive (215) 247-1730, M–F 12–4, 5–9, Sa 10–4, 5–10, Su 10–3, 4–9, reservations strongly recommended, http://www.valleygreeninn.com, food sales.

Weavers Way Co-operative Association, 559 Carpenters Lane (215) 843-2350, M–Th 10–8, F 9–8, Sa–Su 9–6, http://www.weaversway .org, food sales for members only.

Chestnut Hill

DISTANCE: 7.9 miles, 12.8 km

TERRAIN: Moderately hilly. Paved roads with light traffic, except one short section on Germantown Avenue where I suggest you walk your bike.

START: Chestnut Hill Academy on Willow Grove Avenue between Cherokee Street and Huron Road.

ACCESS BY CAR: From I-76 take the Lincoln Drive exit. Follow signs to Lincoln Drive. Continue on Lincoln Drive for 4 miles to the end at the "T" and turn left on Allens Lane. Turn right in 0.4 mile onto McCallum Street. Bear right in 0.5 mile at the stop sign onto Mermaid Lane. Turn left at the next corner at the stop sign onto Cherokee Street. Turn right at the stop sign in 0.2 mile onto Willow Grove Avenue. Chestnut Hill Academy is on the right. There is parking on Willow Grove Avenue.

ACCESS BY PUBLIC TRANSPORTATION: Take **SEPTA Regional Rail Line R8 Chestnut Hill West** to the St. Martins Station. With your back to the station, turn right and go to Willow Grove Avenue and turn left. Chestnut Hill Academy is on the left in 0.2 mile.

SERVICES: There are several spots for lunch or snacks near Germantown Avenue and Bethlehem Pike near mile 2.5. Public restrooms at the train stations on Willow Grove Avenue (about 0.5 mile), Gravers Lane (2.5 miles), and Chestnut Hill Avenue (2.55 miles).

BIKE SHOP: **Wissahickon Cyclery,** 7837 Germantown Avenue (215) 248-2829 (two blocks to the right on Germantown Avenue at mile 8.5).

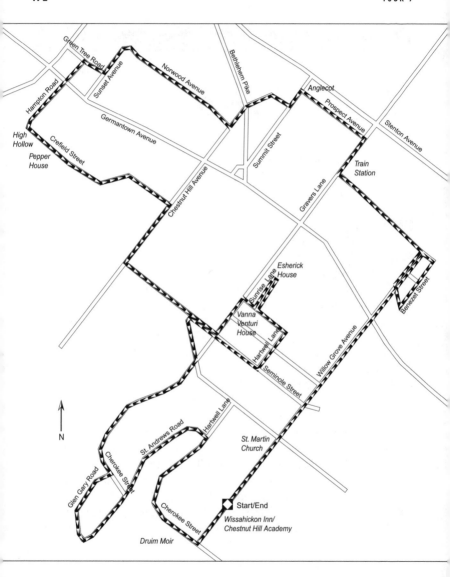

Green Tree Road

Hampton Road

Sunset Avenue

Norwood Avenue

Bethlehem Pike

Anglecot

Prospect Avenue

Stenton Avenue

Germantown Avenue

Summit Street

High Hollow

Crefield Street

Pepper House

Train Station

Chestnut Hill Avenue

Gravers Lane

Esherick House

Sunrise Lane

Benezet Street

Vanna Venturi House

Hartwell Lane

Willow Grove Avenue

Seminole Street

N

St. Andrews Road

Hartwell Lane

St. Martin Church

Glen Gary Road

Cherokee Street

◆ Start/End

Cherokee Street

Wissahickon Inn/ Chestnut Hill Academy

Druim Moir

Until the middle of the nineteenth century the area now known as Chestnut Hill was mostly rural with a few scattered large estates. The arrival of not one but two railroad lines in the 1880s changed that almost immediately. Under the influence of James Gowen, the Reading Railroad came to Chestnut Hill during the 1870s and 1880s, and Henry Howard Houston brought the Pennsylvania Railroad here in 1884. From that time on, Chestnut Hill has attracted residents looking for a bit of the suburbs in the city.

The ride begins at the Chestnut Hill Academy, once the Wissahickon Inn and the first step in Henry Houston's plans to develop his three

CHESTNUT HILL ACADEMY, ORIGINALLY WISSAHICKON INN, WILLOW GROVE AVENUE AND CHEROKEE STREET

thousand acres of land. After Houston's death, his son-in-law George Woodward continued its development and built more diverse housing. You will see part of his "Cotswold village" and some of his homes for the middle class. The route passes homes in East Chestnut Hill that predate Houston and some twentieth-century homes. Chestnut Hill was one of the last neighborhoods in Philadelphia to be developed, so you will see homes in contemporary styles, including a few of international note.

Today, Chestnut Hill is one of Philadelphia's most prosperous neighborhoods; however, this has not always been the case. Departure of more affluent families and development of the western suburbs left the area downtrodden by the late 1960s. Local residents and businesses formed the Chestnut Hill Business Association and the Chestnut Hill Historical Society, both devoted to the revitalization of Germantown Avenue and the surrounding area, and still active and influential.

0.0   Facing Chestnut Hill Academy, go left on Willow Grove Avenue toward Germantown Avenue.

In 1851, thirty-year-old Henry Howard Houston arrived in Philadelphia to work as the general freight agent of the Pennsylvania Railroad. Houston was an ambitious, self-educated businessman, and the railroad became one of the most successful freight transporters in the country under his management. During the Civil War, Houston and other Pennsylvania Railroad associates founded the Union Freight Line that made them rich. Houston's income in 1860 was $5,000. In 1865, it was $114,000. He used his new wealth to buy three thousand acres of mostly contiguous property on the west side of Germantown Avenue and called the area Wissahickon Heights. Included in the property were the ruins of a rustic hunting lodge that had enjoyed some success before it burned down in 1877. On this site Houston constructed the Wissahickon Inn, a luxury resort with 250 rooms and enough stable space for ninety horses and their rigs. The inn was designed by Houston's favorite architects, G. W. and W. D. Hewitt. The Hewitt brothers continued to design homes for Houston, most in the Queen Anne style that was popular at the time. A wide porch surrounded the hotel, which included several dining rooms, a ballroom, and several special areas for smoking, playing cards, reading, and other pastimes. The plan was to entice wealthy Philadelphians to the resort and then convince them to move to the houses Houston was building. It was an enormous success at the expense of the inn. As more people moved into the area, it became less appealing as a rustic lodge, and by 1898 Chestnut Hill Academy took over the property and remains here today.

Just past Chestnut Hill Academy on the left side of Willow Grove Avenue is the **Philadelphia Cricket Club**. This enterprise was initiated by Houston to make sure his guests and future renters were entertained.

St. Martins in the Field Episcopal Church, designed in 1888 by the Hewitts, is also on the left next to the cricket club, at the corner of St. Martins Lane and Willow Grove Avenue. An Episcopalian church was preferred by Houston because it was the religious choice of the upper class at the time. In 2001 the congregation renovated the church and found elaborate polychromatic paint and wallpaper that had been painted white in the 1950s.

By 1881, Houston was named director of the Pennsylvania Railroad, giving him the influence necessary to have the railroad extended to the middle of his holdings. St. Martins station was built a quarter of a mile from the Wissahickon Inn on the right side of Willow Grove Avenue. The inn opened on May 30, 1884, and the railroad made its first run two weeks later.

Houston held his houses for rent rather than for sale. This gave him more control over the development of the overall community. He preferred renting to upper-class white families of native-born Americans, believing this would ensure that his community would remain prosperous.

When Houston died in 1895, his son-in-law George Woodward continued the development of the family properties, building another 180 houses. Although Houston built homes mostly in conventional styles, Woodward experimented, building enclaves that resembled an English countryside village and a medieval hamlet in Normandy (French Village, Tour 8).

From Navaho Street to a block or so after Lincoln Drive, you will see **Woodward's Cotswold Village** on both sides of Willow Grove Avenue. Woodward was inspired on a trip to London's Hyde Park and constructed these homes, most of which are still owned by the Woodward family.

0.85　Straight across Germantown Avenue.

Most of the buildings on Germantown Avenue are commercial, but there are a few residences, including the home and garden of Dr. Peter Hedrick at 8018, to your left on this side of the avenue. The garden was selected by *Good Morning America* as the best garden in the country in 2001, and the public is welcome to visit if the front gate is open. The formal garden has sculpture, fountains, trellises, and benches as focal points amid the brilliant colors and lush foliage arranged in geometric patterns.

1.0　Right on Winston Way.

1.05　Next right on Benezet Street.

Woodward was interested in creating a complete community instead of just renting to the upper class as his father-in-law had done. He developed **Benezet Street** for middle-income families. These charming four-family houses were built between 1910 and 1916. They are still owned and rented by the Woodward family. Not surprisingly, there is a long waiting list.

1.2　Right on Germantown Avenue.

The business district along Germantown Avenue is thriving, although this has not always been the case. The Chestnut Hill Business Association has been very active through the years in promoting business practices that will enhance the area as a whole. They exert a great deal of pressure on businesses to conform to fairly rigid specifications for type of business as well as the appearance of buildings. Several merchants have been dissuaded from opening shops on Germantown Avenue, and others have entered long discussions about what signs, colors, or display windows were appropriate. In general, the business association has tried to promote small, upscale shops and restaurants. Chain stores and fast food have faced stiff opposition. You will find some of these along the avenue, but they have all made major concessions to the business association. Some businesses and residents believe the association is too rigid and conservative, but others laud the organization for rescuing the business district and continuing to keep it strong while other neighborhood main streets struggle.

Shop owners have also needed to adapt to changes from outside the community. An old trolley stop at the corner of Germantown Avenue and Cresheim Valley Drive, to the left, was converted to a flower shop after the trolley was discontinued. To the right, O'Donnell's Stationery Store was a mainstay of Chestnut Hill for decades until the arrival of large office supply chain stores. O'Donnell's made a smooth transition to O'Doodles, a delightful and successful children's store, selling unusual toys, arts and crafts, and clothing.

1.25 Right on Willow Grove Avenue.

1.35 Left on Winston Way.

1.4 Left on Ardleigh Street.

In this section of East Chestnut Hill, many of the early twentieth-century residents were Irish, Italian, and German immigrants. The Water Tower Recreation Center on the right sponsors programs for children and adults, including an amateur theater company.

2.0 Right on Gravers Lane.

In 0.15 mile, stop at Gravers Station Road before the bridge over the railroad tracks and look to the right at the **Gravers Lane Train Station**. This is the Chestnut Hill East train line, once part of the Reading Railroad.

In 1792, Joseph Miller built a house on his large farm in what is now East Mount Airy. His daughter, Mary, her husband James Gowen, and their children moved into it in 1794. Gowen expanded the property and his heirs broke apart the estate, selling off parcels of land for development as upper-class homes. In the face of competition from Houston for migrating city dwellers, the Gowens looked for ways to entice people to their properties. They employed Frank Furness to design train stations for the Reading line. The tower and turret of the Gravers Lane Station are classic Furness designs with multipitched roofs and unusually shaped dormers.

2.25 Left on Prospect Avenue.

Anglecot is the large house with a sundial on the front one block down on the right at the intersection of Evergreen and Prospect Avenues. Built in 1883 and designed by noted architect Wilson Eyre, it was the home of Charles Adam Potter, whose wealth came from manufacturing oilcloth and linoleum. Eyre was twenty-five when he designed this home in Queen Anne style, which was created by Scottish architect Richard Norman Shaw and first seen in this country during the 1876 Centennial Exposition in Fairmount Park (Tour 6). Over the next twenty years Eyre altered Anglecot many times. Eyre's tastes changed during those years from the ornate Victorian style of the original to the more sedate Arts and Crafts style. The building has been divided in co-ops, an increasingly common way to fit large older buildings into modern lifestyles. In this case, the façade has been preserved and the house looks much like it did the last time Eyre remodeled.

2.5 Left on Summit Avenue.

The large white house on the right at the corner of Prospect and Summit Avenues at **100 Summit Avenue** is one of the earliest homes in Chestnut Hill. It was built in Victorian Italianate style in 1856 for George Watson, a carriagemaker, and predates the arrival of the railroad.

2.55 Right on Chestnut Hill Avenue immediately after crossing the railroad bridge.

This is the final station on the Chestnut Hill East train line.

ITALIANATE HOUSE ON SUMMIT AVENUE

2.7 Straight across Bethlehem Pike. Chestnut Hill Avenue bends
slightly to the left.

To the left on Bethlehem Pike, the Chestnut Hill West train station and
the heart of the business community is near the intersection of Bethlehem Pike and Germantown Avenue. The Chestnut Hill Historical Society (M–F 9–5) at 8708 Germantown Avenue and the Visitor's Center
(M–F 8:30–4, Sa 10–3) at 8425 are a few blocks away. Both were
established in the 1960s, and both sponsor lectures and tours and have
exhibits about the community. The historical society manages a jointly
sponsored land easement program that has won several awards and
aims at saving key historic structures. Owners of properties within the
Wissahickon Creek watershed are eligible for tax deductible donations
of development rights to the historical society. This prevents the subdi-
vision or development of the property and the alteration of the building façade by subsequent owners.

2.8 Right on Norwood Avenue.

There are several large old homes along these streets. The **Norwood-Fortbone Academy** is at the end of Norwood Avenue. It is run by the Sisters of St. Joseph and was established in 1920.

3.2 Left on Sunset Avenue.

3.3 Right on Green Tree Road.

A handsome pair of stone Chinese lions guard the front of the estate on the corner of Green Tree and Hampton Roads.

3.4 Left on Hampton Road.

3.5 Straight across Germantown Avenue.

From here to Chestnut Hill Avenue in about a mile, you will see some beautiful homes patterned after medieval English and French country homes. This style was popular during the first quarter of the twentieth century, when wealthy Americans wanted homes that were reminiscent of English manor houses.

  High Hollow is at the end of Hampton Road on a private cul-de-sac, so unfortunately you can only see a bit of it. George Howe, one of country's most popular architects of the country manor style, designed the house for himself in 1914. Howe was especially popular among bankers, causing him to refer to his work as Wall Street Pastoral. Howe was noted for accurate reproductions that included pre-sagged roofs and weathered walls. Like his own home, the houses were rustic and opulent at the same time. Ironically, Howe is best remembered for designing the PSFS Building, the first International-style skyscraper in America (Tour 3).

3.65 Follow the road to the left where it becomes Crefeld Street.

The **Pepper House** is at 9120 Crefeld Street on the right, next to High Hollow. This house was designed in 1920 by Willing and Sims, who were among the most successful in the medieval revival genre. The **Scofield Andrews House** is also on the right at 9002 Crefeld Street and was designed in 1930. This is a particularly impressive enclave of medieval-style buildings surrounded by a stone wall.

4.25 Right on Chestnut Hill Avenue.

4.45 Left on Seminole Street.

Houston's daughter Gertrude is credited with convincing her father to name the streets in Wissahickon Heights after American Indian nations. Others chosen included Navaho, Cherokee, Pocono, Huron, Roanoke, and Shawnee.

4.9 Left on Gravers Lane.

5.0 Right on Millman Place.

There is a driveway on the right for the **Vanna Venturi House** at 8330 Millman Place opposite Sunrise Lane. You can just see the house at the end. Postmodernist guru Robert Venturi built this house for his mother, Vanna, in 1962. Although Vanna never liked the house, it brought national attention to Venturi, who went on to exert a profound influence on international architecture, leading the move away from International style toward postmodernism.

In the 1880s, Houston had houses designed in ornate Queen Anne style, which borrowed elements from such older European styles as Gothic and Romanesque. The pendulum swings back and forth in architecture as in other artistic expressions, and the next generation came to loathe the gewgaws and clutter of the Victorians. The 1920s saw the birth of International style with the Bauhaus school of architecture. Ornamental details were rejected, leaving the façades sleek and smooth. International-style architects did not use any decorative elements that invoked the past. The style echoed the contemporary philosophy that the future was bright and there was no need to look back. Most of the skyscrapers in this country are in the International style. With another swing of the pendulum, postmodernists brought back color, decoration, and historical elements such as columns and pediments. Postmodern elements are more minimalist and abstract, and the lines are cleaner and less elaborate than their nineteenth-century predecessors.

5.05 Left on Sunrise Lane.

Louis I. Kahn designed the house at **204 Sunrise Lane** for Margaret Esherick in 1960. Kahn was an influential architect whose signature style has been dubbed the Philadelphia School. In many ways it is an intermediate between the International and postmodern styles. Robert Venturi was Kahn's student at the University of Pennsylvania, and Kahn had a profound effect on Venturi as a young man.

Kahn was educated and taught at the University of Pennsylvania and designed the Richards Medical Building (Tour 10), which he considered to be his most important work. He designed several residential buildings, but the Esherick House is one of the few actually constructed.

ESHERICK HOUSE ON SUNRISE LANE

5.15 Ride around the circle at the end of Sunrise Lane and go back to Millman Place.

5.25 Left on Millman Place.

There are only a few houses in the Philadelphia area designed in the International style. One is the **Charles Woodward House** at 8220 Millman Place, the white house with the wrought-iron door. It was designed in 1939 by Kenneth Day, son of the prominent nineteenth-century Victorian architect Frank Miles Day.

5.4 Right on Hartwell Lane.

5.55 Right on Seminole Street.

Among the hundred or so houses that Henry Houston built is the one at **8205 Seminole Street,** on the corner of Seminole Street and Hartwell Lane. Unlike most of the others, Houston sold this house rather than holding it for rent.

5.9 Left on St. Martins Lane.

6.1 Right on Gravers Lane.

The golf course on the left is part of the Philadelphia Cricket Club, which you saw earlier on the ride. The woods on the right are owned by private estates.

6.4 The road bends to the left and becomes Cherokee Street.

6.5 Right on Glen Gary Road.

This section of Chestnut Hill is strictly twentieth century with some huge homes and modern estates.

Artist and author Dorothy Shipley White built the house on the right at **717 Glen Gary Road** in 1963. It was designed by Mitchell/Giurgola Associates, one of Philadelphia's best-known architectural firms. The rear of the house overlooks Wissahickon Gorge and is mostly faced with glass for an unobstructed view.

6.7 Follow the road to the left where it becomes St. Andrews Road.

7.3   Right at the "T" onto Hartwell Lane.

The main building of the Philadelphia Cricket Club is on the left up ahead.

7.5   Follow the road to the left where it joins Cherokee Street.

Houston built a home for himself in 1885 on fifty-five acres of land near the Wissahickon Inn. **Springside**, the private school on the right, was built on a part of the estate. Behind the school **Druim Moir**, or "great crag" in Scottish Gaelic, still stands. A veritable castle above the bluffs of the Wissahickon Gorge, it was designed by the Hewitts.

In the 1940s, the family gave the house to the Presbyterian Church as a home for retired clergy. But the building was too expensive for the church to maintain, and the family regained ownership. It was remodeled and today contains three condominiums. Much effort was expended to maintain as much of the façade as possible, and the estate remains in common ownership to assure a unified look.

7.75   Left at the stop sign onto Willow Grove Avenue.

7.85   End at Chestnut Hill Academy.

ATTRACTIONS IN CHESTNUT HILL

Chestnut Hill Historical Society, 8708 Germantown Avenue (215) 247-0417, M–F 9–5, www.chhist.org, free.

Visitor's Center, 8426 Germantown Avenue (215) 247-6696, M–F 8:30–4, Sa 10–3, http://www.chestnuthillpa.com, free.

University City and the Streetcar Suburbs

DISTANCE: 9 miles, 14.6 km

TERRAIN: Flat. Paved roads, a few with some traffic. There are four short sections on walkways. You can ride on them in the evening and on weekends, but you should walk your bike during the day on weekdays. Also, walk on the sidewalk around the post office and train station to avoid traffic.

START: The center of the University of Pennsylvania campus at Thirty-fourth and Walnut Streets.

ACCESS BY CAR: Take I-76 to the Thirtieth Street exit. Follow Market Street west and turn left on Thirty-fourth Street. There is parking on the street at meters around Walnut Street, where the ride begins.

ACCESS BY PUBLIC TRANSPORTATION: All **SEPTA Regional Rail Lines** and the **Market/Frankford High Speed Line** stop at Amtrak's Thirtieth Street Station at Market and Thirtieth Streets. Ride west four blocks to Thirty-fourth Street. Turn left and ride two blocks south to Walnut Street.

SERVICES: Food and drinks are available along Spruce Street (mile 0.3 and 0.6) and in the train station (mile 8.2). There are food trucks in front of the Hospital of the University of Pennsylvania and on Spruce Street at Thirty-sixth Street during the day on weekdays. Public restrooms are at the post office and train station (mile 8.2).

BIKE SHOPS: **Bike Line of University City,** 226 South 40th Street (215) 243-2453 (to the left on Fortieth Street at mile 4.3), and **Astrobike,** 3620 Lancaster Avenue (215) 222-3480 (mile 5.2).

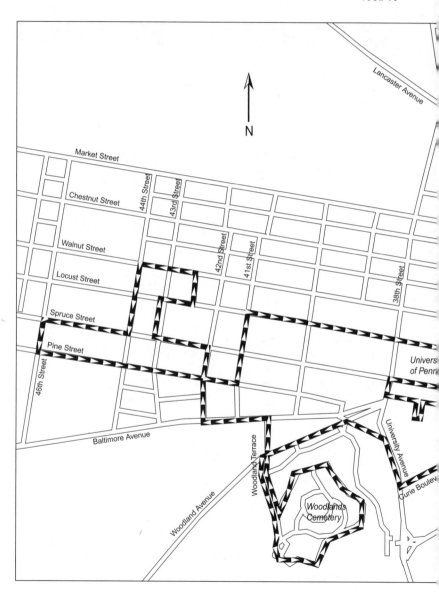

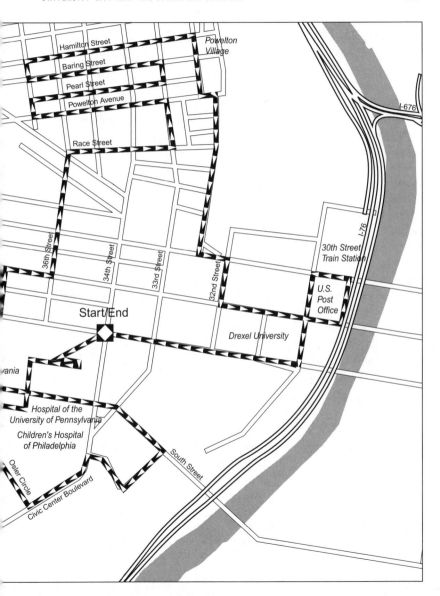

The ride begins in front of College Hall on the campus of the University of Pennsylvania. After a short tour of the campus, you will ride through two of America's earliest suburbs: Spruce Hill to the west and Powelton Village to the north of the university. The arrival of streetcars in West Philadelphia brought wealthy speculators and a new merchant class to the neighborhood in the mid-1800s. These areas remained prosperous until the mid-1900s, when many families moved to western suburbs and properties were neglected. Today there is renewed interest in the surviving original Victorian houses, and both Spruce Hill and Powelton Village are experiencing dramatic growth.

Also in University City is Drexel University, established by nineteenth-century entrepreneur and philanthropist Anthony J. Drexel. On this ride, you'll see Drexel University's oldest and newest buildings. The tour concludes with a loop around two of Philadelphia's few Art Deco buildings: Philadelphia's main post office and train station, both at Thirtieth and Market Streets.

0.0   Begin at Thirty-fourth and Walnut Streets. Go along the paved walkway diagonally to the southwest. Bicycles must be walked from 8 A.M. to 5 P.M. on weekdays, but you may ride evenings and weekends.

You will pass a large, black, abstract sculpture on your left. The sculpture is *Black Forest or Polyhedron Forms* by Robinson Friendenthal, installed in 1977. This section of campus is **Blanche Levy Park.**

The University of Pennsylvania was founded in 1740 when a group of working-class Philadelphians started collecting funds to construct the "New Building," planned to be a preaching hall, a charity school for poor children, and the largest building in the city. Unable to collect enough money, construction was halted for nearly ten years. In 1749, Benjamin Franklin published a pamphlet titled "Proposals for the Education of Youth in Pennsylvania," which advocated the first secular school in the colonies to be called the "Publick Academy of Philadelphia." At that time, Harvard, Yale, and Princeton were seminaries.

Franklin assembled a twenty-four-member board of directors who completed the building, and the first classes began in 1751 at Fourth and Arch Streets. In 1755, the name was changed to the College of Philadelphia, and in 1765 the school added the first medical school in the colonies, established by surgeon John Morgan. Continental army troops were housed on campus in 1775, and classes were suspended until 1779, when the school reopened as the University of the State of Pennsylvania, the country's first. The university outgrew the original building and moved to Ninth and Chestnut Streets in 1802. Seventy years later, it moved to this location.

0.1   Stop in front of **College Hall.**

College Hall was the first building on this campus, designed by Thomas W. Richards. With a brownstone base, greenstone walls, and polished red granite pillars, it is easy to recognize. At the time, Richards was an instructor in mechanical drawing at the university and won a competition to design College Hall. The board was so impressed with the plans that Richards was promoted to professor and asked to design three more buildings, including **Logan Hall** to the right, which was renovated in the 1990s. Richards became the university's first professor of architecture.

The sculpture **Benjamin Franklin** is located in front of College Hall. The statue was created in 1899 by John J. Boyle, a prominent sculptor in nineteenth-century Philadelphia. It was originally located at the post office at Ninth and Chestnut Street and was donated by the city to the university in 1938.

Split Button is opposite Benjamin Franklin and is the 1981 work of Claes Oldenburg and Coosje van Bruggen. Oldenburg also created *Clothespin* located outside City Hall (Tour 3). Oldenburg likes to make monuments out of small everyday objects. The idea for *Split Button* came from Ben's vest. Oldenburg imagined that it might be missing a button, and then imagined the button breaking due to the stress of holding Franklin's generous girth in place.

As you face *Split Button* with Ben at your back, turn to your right and proceed toward an orange metal sculpture at the end of the mall.

Jerusalem Stabile was created by Alexander Calder, the youngest of three generations of acclaimed sculptors from Philadelphia (Tour 3).

0.15 Stop at the large ornate red brick building to the right.

This is the **Anne and Jerome Fisher Fine Arts Library** (Tu–F 10–5, Sa–Su 12–5), designed by Frank Furness in 1888 and restored in 1991. The building was one of the most innovative libraries of its day. The walls on the outside of the stacks were constructed to allow them to be removed with jackscrews so that an addition could be placed without disrupting the original design. There are translucent glass floors in the stacks to allow light to filter through the skylights on the roof. The reading room has alcoves lit from above and a huge fireplace.

ANNE AND JEROME FISHER FINE ARTS LIBRARY, UNIVERSITY OF PENNSYLVANIA

Furness was immensely popular at the height of his career, and he is now recognized as one of America's best architects. He was one of few American architects of his time who did not study at the Ecole des Beaux-Arts in Paris. In fact, Furness did not travel outside of the United States at all but learned from local architects and from photographs. This seeming deficit may be the ultimate reason for his innovative style.

Furness's façades were controversial, even at the height of his popularity. He used oversized columns and pillars decorated with natural motifs. His buildings are colorful, mixing colored bricks, terra-cotta, and tiles on façades. There are also turrets, gables, and various sculptural elements such as gargoyles and elaborate brackets. Even admirers consider his work a bit bizarre, but for those of us who love his buildings, the eccentricity is part of the joy.

The building was restored in 1991 by Venturi, Scott Brown and Associates, one of Philadelphia's most prestigious architectural firms. Robert Venturi was one of the first influential architects to recognize Furness's genius and was his most vocal supporter, especially when high Victorian style was out of favor. The university would have razed the library without Venturi's influence.

The **Arthur Ross Gallery** (Tu–F 10–5, Sa–Su 12–5) is inside the Fine Arts Library, established in 1983 in a 1920s addition to the main library. It is open to the public. The exhibits change regularly and feature visual arts, including paintings, sculpture, prints, and textiles.

Turn around and continue through campus past College Hall.

0.25 Left at the Thirty-sixth Street walkway toward the traffic light on Spruce Street.

0.3 Cross Spruce Street at the light and continue straight.

The huge burnt brick and limestone buildings on your right, once called the **Men's Dormitories,** are the **Quadrangle Dorms**, the first section of which was built from 1895 to 1902 by Cope and Stewardson. Cope and Stewardson designed a total of nine university buildings between 1892 and 1912 and are credited with providing the University of Pennsylvania with a unified architectural look. Even today new buildings have brick façades and white trim like these buildings. These dorms were inspired by residential colleges in England and were designed to be built in stages without looking incomplete. Four additions were built between 1905 and 1928 in a rambling plan with courtyards of different sizes and shapes. The four entrance gates were each built in a different style. Be sure to look at the gargoyles above you all around the building. They are fanciful and alternately fearsome and humorous.

0.35 Right on Hamilton Walk.

You can continue to look at the gargoyles on the Quad on the right. On this side, athletes are represented in uniforms and holding the equipment of their sport.

   The University of Pennsylvania Medical School is on the left. The second building on the left is the **John Morgan Building**, named after school's founder. At Thirty-seventh and Hamilton Walk, you will see the **Richards Medical Building**. This, along with the Furness library, is among the university's architectural treasures. It was built from 1957 to 1961 by Louis I. Kahn and is considered one of the most significant buildings in modern American architecture. The Richards Medical Building was a pivotal project in Kahn's illustrious career and marked the beginning of the style now known as the Philadelphia School.

            The core tower contains service elevators, utilities, and animal facilities, leaving open space on the outside for labs. Inside, concrete beams are exposed, allowing even more open area and allowing for easy connections to utilities. These innovations are still in use for modern laboratory facilities. However, Kahn's designs were ahead of many contemporary technologies. The labs were, and still are, difficult to keep cool in summer and warm in winter. Also, the exposed cinderblock construction and monochromatic interiors are considered a bit depressing by those who work in them every day.

0.5   Immediately after the Richards Medical Building, follow a pathway to the left to the **Biopond**.

At the first gravel path, turn left again and continue to the pond. This

RICHARDS MEDICAL BUILDING FROM THE BIOPOND, UNIVERSITY OF PENNSYLVANIA

is a well-hidden garden spot open to the public from dawn to dusk, and many folks who live in the area, or even work here, don't know about it. The Biopond was established in 1897 on five acres of land as a research botanical garden. Construction of the medical buildings and Thirty-eighth Street forced it into this much smaller space, and today there is little academic work here, but it remains a delightful place to visit.

0.51 Go back to Hamilton Walk and continue to the left.

0.55 Right on Thirty-eighth Street.

0.6 Right on Spruce Street.

On the left just before Thirty-fourth Street is **Irvine Auditorium**, designed by Horace Trumbauer in 1929.

The Hospital of the University of Pennsylvania is on the right at this corner. This is one of the leading teaching hospitals in the country.

The **University of Pennsylvania Museum of Archaeology and Anthropology** (Tu–Sa 10–4:30, Su 1–5) is on the right after you cross Thirty-third Street. In the late nineteenth century, the University of Pennsylvania accumulated a huge collection of art and architecture from several expeditions to Egypt that it sponsored and set aside twelve acres on this site for its expanding archaeology department. Egyptology was popular at the time, and the discovery of Tutankhamun's tomb in 1922 accelerated the craze. Philadelphia's leading artists and artisans were employed to contribute to this Arts and Crafts-style building, which opened in 1926. Wilson Eyre was the primary architect, with contributions by Frank Miles Day. Nicola D'Ascenzo created stained glass art and Henry Chapman Mercer made the tiles. Ironwork was by Samuel Yellin, the great modern hand-wrought ironworker. Most of the carved work is by Alexander Milne Calder (Tour 3). If the gate is open to the entrance farthest from Thirty-third Street, walk around the courtyard. The four gatepost sculptures represent Africa, America, Europe, and Asia, in harmony with the museum contents. The museum's collections are extensive, and there are galleries devoted to the world's great civilizations. They also sponsor concerts and lectures, bringing performers and experts from around the world.

1.15 Right on Convention Center Avenue.

1.4 Left on Thirty-fourth Street/Civic Center Boulevard.

The **Children's Hospital of Philadelphia (CHOP)** is straight ahead of you. The semicircular section on the left is CHOP's newest building. The **Hospital of the University of Pennsylvania (HUP)** occupies the buildings to the right.

1.55 Right on Osler Circle.

This is the **medical research center** of CHOP and the University of Pennsylvania. Collectively, these laboratories, all built in the past twenty years, form one of the top research facilities in the country.

1.7   Left on Curie Boulevard.

1.85 Right on University Avenue/Thirty-eighth Street. READ THE NEXT SET OF DIRECTIONS TO WOODLAND AVENUE BEFORE CONTINUING.

2.0   Left at the second light on Baltimore Avenue. Use the crosswalk rather than hazarding the left-turn lanes.

2.05 Bear left at the next light onto Woodland Avenue. The road splits here and you want to take the left fork. The bike lane continues on Baltimore Avenue, and you will need to leave the bike lane and move across traffic. There is a traffic light at Thirty-ninth Street where you can cross Baltimore Avenue and then turn right onto Woodland Avenue.

2.25 Left into the **Woodlands Cemetery**.

The Woodlands Cemetery (M–Th 9–5) was once the estate of Andrew Hamilton, a lawyer and architect of Independence Hall (Tour 1). The original house (M–Th 10–3) was one of the finest Federal-style mansions in Philadelphia when it was built in 1742. Hamilton's grandson created one of America's earliest English romantic gardens here. The estate was converted to a cemetery in 1843.

The Victorians had a fascination with death and the passage to the next world. They came to cemeteries for picnics and to roam among the graves. An impressive tomb was an important status symbol, and they spent as much as they could afford on cemetery art. Toward the end of the nineteenth century, when Egyptology was the rage, an obelisk was chosen to honor George Washington in the nation's capital, and others followed by choosing an obelisk as their own monument. You can spend some time riding through the cemetery if you like before returning to Woodland Avenue.

2.28 Go back to Woodland Avenue and turn left.

2.3   Right on **Woodland Terrace**.

The area from Woodland Avenue north to Chestnut Street and from about Fortieth Street to about Forty-sixth Street is known as Spruce Hill.

Horse-drawn trolley cars made their way from Center City across the Schuylkill River into West Philadelphia in 1860, opening up the previously rural farmland to development. At the same time, a new middle class emerged from the economic boom that followed the end of the Civil War, looking for elegant but moderately priced housing outside of the city. Real estate barons built many homes on speculation here and rented or sold the properties to accommodate the new suburbanites.

West Philadelphia suffered economic depression in the mid-twentieth century but began a renaissance toward the end of the century that is in full swing today. You will see magnificently renovated mansions as well as those in need of work. You will also see new residential and commercial buildings.

The Victorians rebelled against the strict symmetry of the colonial-era Georgian and Federal styles. They were naturalists and wanted homes with odd lines, many facets, and a rambling appearance, which they considered to be more harmonious with an uncultivated landscape. Gardens became less formal and less manicured. Irregularly shaped ponds replaced fountains, and free-form shrubs replaced topiaries and clipped hedges. The Victorians were also nostalgic and revived most of the major European architectural styles, sometimes all in the same building. The homes on Woodland Terrace are Italianate, recognizable from the squared-off rooflines and the square towers, or lanterns, on the top. All of the houses are twins built in 1861 by Samuel Sloane, one of the country's most respected Victorian architects and author of two popular pattern books.

More visible to the buying public, the houses at either end of Woodland Terrace are larger and grander than those in the middle. The end houses are built of stone while the middle homes are stucco or softer inexpensive brownstone. All of the houses have a front garden or terrace separating the building from the street, a fairly new concept at the time.

The historic marker on this street notes that Paul Philippe Cret lived here. Cret was an urban planner and designed the Franklin Parkway, among other projects.

2.35 Left on Baltimore Avenue.

2.45 Right on Forty-second Street.

Horace Trumbauer designed the mansion on the corner of **Forty-second and Pine Streets**. Today it is the location of the University of Pennsylvania Press.

2.6 Left on Spruce Street.

The **Philadelphia Divinity School** is on the right at the corner of Forty-second and Spruce Streets, built from 1925 to 1926 in Gothic revival style.

The fantastic row of homes on the left, from **4206** to **4218 Spruce Street,** is attributed to G. W. and W. D. Hewitt (Tour 9). Built in 1883, they are in Queen Anne style recognizable by the scrollwork porches and painted trim.

The **University City Arts League,** on the left at 4226 Spruce Street, was established in 1967 by a small group of local artists who wanted to offer informal classes in arts and crafts. Today there are more than four thousand members who can choose from seventy-five classes and workshops on fine arts, crafts, languages, writing, music, and dance.

The **Sadie Tanner Mossell Alexander University of Pennsylvania Partnership School,** on the right on this block, held its first classes in September 2001 and is open to neighborhood children in grades pre-K to 8. The University of Pennsylvania's Graduate School of Education worked with the Philadelphia public school system to develop the curriculum and design the school using innovative theories and techniques, and the university is also supporting the school financially.

In the 1980s and 1990s, members of the University City community, which includes some four thousand University of Pennsylvania employees, convinced the university to become more involved with the neighborhood. More than a decade of effort has resulted in such partnerships as this school. The university has contributed funds, labor, and training to many civic organizations, instituted programs to assist residents in education and child care, and extended university services, such as security and street cleaning, beyond university borders. They also offer grants to university employees who move into or make improvements to homes in University City.

2.75 Right on Forty-third Street.

2.85 Right on Locust Street.

2.95 Left on **St. Mark's Place**.

The black trim on these red-brick row houses gives them mystery and grace. They are believed to have been designed by the Hewitt brothers.

3.0 Left on Walnut Street. Stay on the left side of Walnut Street, which is one-way to the west, as you will be turning left in a block and a half.

The **Restaurant School** is across the street on Walnut in a converted Victorian mansion once owned by John Wanamaker, Philadelphia's largest retailer. The school offers a full curriculum of courses on fine cooking and the restaurant industry and operates an excellent restaurant that is open to the public daily for dinner.

3.15 Left on Forty-fourth Street.

3.3 Right on Spruce Street.

3.5 Left on Forty-sixth Street.

3.6 Left on **Pine Street**.

Pine Street is lined with brightly painted houses in Queen Anne style.

4.05 Left on Forty-first Street.

4.2 Right on Locust Street.

4.3 Continue straight onto the campus of the University of Pennsylvania where Locust Street becomes **Locust Walk**.

You can ride your bike on this pathway on weekends and after 5 P.M. on weekdays. At other times you must walk your bike.

The mammoth orange steel sculpture on Locust Walk is *Covenant* by Alexander Lieberman, depicting the staying of Abraham's sacrifice of his son. In the mid-1960s a survey listed the amount of outdoor art on college campuses in the country. The University of Pennsylvania was near the bottom, creating embarrassment and a flurry of acquisitional activity. As a result, styles popular in the 1970s are well represented on campus.

The Kelly Writers House is just past *Covenant* on the left. After World War II, the university expanded across Thirty-eighth Street, and many houses were razed to accommodate new buildings. This thirteen-room house at 3805 Locust Walk survived to become a meeting place for lectures, readings, and support groups by and for writers.

Ride over Thirty-eighth Street. The elevation of the bridge provides a good view of the campus to the west. **Huntsman Hall,** the cylindrical behemoth to the left on Thirty-eighth Street, is the newest addition to the Wharton School, the University of Pennsylvania's internationally renowned business school. Wharton conducted more than one hundred focus groups of students, faculty, and administrators to design the state-of-the-art academic building, which opened in 2002. Jon M. Huntsman, a Wharton graduate, businessman, and philanthropist, and his family have contributed some $50 million to the university.

On the right at Thirty-seventh Street you can share a seat with a sculpture of Benjamin Franklin sitting on a bench reading a newspaper. It was created by George Lundeen in 1987.

4.65 Left on Thirty-seventh Street.

4.7 Right on Chestnut Street.

International House and **Tabernacle Presbyterian Church** are at the intersection of Thirty-seventh and Chestnut Streets.

International House, on the left, was built in 1970 and is much more than a dormitory for foreign students studying in the area. In 1908, Dr. A. Waldo Stevenson began hosting informal meetings with foreign students in his house in West Philadelphia. Stevenson wanted to create a place where foreign students could relax and share the joys and stresses of adjusting to life in Philadelphia. These meetings became increasingly popular and led to the founding of the International Students House in 1918, the first of its kind in the country. Today, there are eleven hundred students from fifty countries. The International House sponsors concerts, speakers, films, and social events all year designed to support foreign students and make them feel welcome and safe in the city.

Tabernacle Presbyterian Church was built from 1884 to 1886. Today it is the home of Tabernacle United Church and the Iron Gate Theater. Maggie Kuhn and five friends founded the Gray Panthers here in 1970 under the name "Consultation of Older and Younger Adults." Within a year the organization, devoted to the rights of older people, had one hundred members and now is a national organization with headquarters in Washington, D.C.

4.85 Left on Thirty-sixth Street.

5.25 Right on Race Street.

You are entering another historic district known as **Powelton Village**. This area has a similar history to Spruce Hill. The arrival of horse-drawn trolleys from Center City changed it from a rural area to an affluent suburb. Many of the same builders purchased property and constructed speculative housing in both neighborhoods. You will find more Italianate villas along these streets, and some of the city's best Victorian Gothic homes are along Powelton Avenue. Many of these mansions are too large for today's typical families and have been either purchased by fraternities of Drexel University or converted to apartments.

In the 1940s, the area earned a reputation as one of the toughest neighborhoods in Philadelphia, with violent gangs prowling the streets. But the long-term residents were tenacious in their desire to save their homes, and civic organizations sprang up in the 1950s, successfully ousting the gangs. Over the next decade, houses were rented to students, and Powelton became a favorite haunt of left-wing political activists. One of the most notorious of these is Ira Einhorn, who was living at 3411 Race Street with his girlfriend, Holly Maddux, when Maddux disappeared in September 1977. Einhorn was arrested eighteen months later when Holly's mummified body was found stuffed into a trunk in the apartment. Released on bail, Einhorn fled the country before the trial in 1981. It took sixteen years to find him in southern France and another four years to have him extradited. He was convicted of Maddux's murder and sentenced to life in prison in 2002.

5.5   Left on Thirty-third Street.

Frederick Poth was a wealthy brewer who invested heavily and lived in this area. The **Poth Mansion** is on the left at 216 North Thirty-third Street, at the corner of Powelton Avenue.

5.6   Left on Powelton Avenue.

From **Thirty-third to Thirty-fifth Streets** you'll see small red-brick twins with ornately trimmed porches. The ornate scrollwork that we associate with Victorian architecture was made possible by the invention of the jigsaw.

5.9   Right on Thirty-seventh Street.

5.95 Right on Pearl Street.

Some of the old carriage houses along this street have been converted to modern homes.

6.25 Left on Thirty-third Street.

6.35 Left on Baring Street.

You will see more Italianate homes along this street. Wilson Eyre designed the home at **3511 Baring Street** in 1891. Although it was built almost one hundred years later in 1988, the **Gaither House,** across the street at 3601, maintained a Victorian feel while incorporating modern conveniences, such as a two-car garage.

6.65 Right on Thirty-seventh Street.

6.7   Right on Hamilton Street.

7.05   Right on Thirty-second Street.

The neighborhood is now attracting new residents who are interested in modern housing but want to preserve the older charm, resulting in the construction of homes like the ones to the left. The new houses are faced with brick and have overhanging roofs and brackets like their Victorian neighbors.

7.2   Right on Powelton Avenue.

7.25   Quick left to stay on Thirty-second Street.

The campus of **Drexel University** begins on both sides of Thirty-second Street. Anthony J. Drexel, an international financier, philanthropist, and mentor of J. P. Morgan, founded the institution to provide an opportunity for middle- and lower-income students to receive an education in the newly emerging technical trades in art, domestic science, technology, and commerce. The first classes were offered in 1891, one year before Drexel's death. Both sexes and all nationalities were admitted from the beginning, an uncommon policy at that time. Today Drexel University specializes in business and technology, offers undergraduate and graduate degrees, and is a national leader in the development of online education.

7.6   Left on Market Street.

The new **Leonard Pearlstein Business Learning Center** is the handsome brick and blue-glass building where Thirty-second Street ends at Market Street. Designed by architect Phillip Johnson, the center opened in 2002.

7.65   Right at the next light, along the walkway toward Chestnut Street.

The sculpture atop the granite pedestal on your right is **Anthony J. Drexel,** sculpted by Moses Jacob Ezekiel in 1904. It was dedicated by Drexel's granddaughters in 1905. Drexel was also the first president of the Fairmount Park Art Commission, and the statue was originally located within the park at Belmont and Lansdowne Avenues. It was given to Drexel Institute in 1966. Drexel's granddaughter, Mother Katherine Drexel, was elevated to sainthood by the Catholic Church in 2000.

The red-brick building on your left is **Centennial Bank**, designed in 1876 by Frank Furness and renovated in 2000. In the nineteenth century the main depot of the Pennsylvania Railroad was on this corner. This attracted many commercial enterprises to the immediate area. The Centennial Bank is the only one that remains. It is now the Paul Peck Center and part of Drexel University.

7.75 Left on Chestnut Street.

Drexel Institute (M–F 8:30–6, Sa 10–12), the school's original building, is on the corner of Thirty-second and Chestnut Streets. It was built in the elaborate Italian Renaissance style from 1889 to 1891 by the Wilson brothers. One of the brothers, Joseph, also managed the institute. Inside, the central court has rococo red tile, pink marble, and white enameled brick with wrought-iron balustrades and carved pilasters decorated with gold. It is open to the public and worth a stop.

8.05 Left on Schuylkill Expressway frontage road. I recommend getting off the bike and walking along the sidewalk to avoid heavy traffic here.

8.15 Left on Market Street. Continue walking your bike.

There are four majestic granite eagles on the Market Street Bridge. Fourteen of these sculptures were placed on top of Pennsylvania Station in New York City in 1903. When the station was demolished in 1963, these four were given to the Fairmount Park Art Association and were installed here in 1967. The eagles are five feet high and six feet wide. Each one weighs 5,500 pounds.

The main branch of the **U.S. Post Office** (daily 24 hours) in Philadelphia is the Art Deco structure, on your left. Look at the stone carvings and metal details at the entrances. The main lobby is also beautiful.

Amtrak's **Thirtieth Street Station** (daily 24 hours) is on the opposite side of Market Street on your right. The station was built from 1929 to 1934, and restored in 1991. Philadelphia planners wanted to construct a boulevard in the city reminiscent of the Champs-Elysées in Paris (Tour 3). To do this, they razed hundreds of buildings between City Hall and East Fairmount Park. Among the businesses displaced was the Pennsylvania Railroad. In exchange for the land, the city gave the railroad tunnel rights from the Schuylkill River to Fifteenth Street, and the railroad built Suburban and Thirtieth Street Stations on either end. The front of the building faces the Schuylkill River and that is the best view of the enormous Corinthian columns.

If you have the time, lock your bike up and take a look inside the station. The immense waiting area is splendid. The walls are faced with marble, and the huge glass walls at either end allow light to pour across the vast space. There are many classical elements, blended with the then-popular Art Nouveau to give a stately but stylish appearance. The station originally held a chapel, a mortuary, three thousand square feet of hospital space and a landing deck for aircraft. The **Pennsylvania Railroad War Memorial** is at the far end of the waiting area. It was created in 1950 by Walter Hancock and dedicated to railroad workers who lost their lives in World War II. Michael the Archangel is lifting the body of a soldier, freeing him from battle. The names of all 1,307 railroad employees who died in World War II are listed on the pedestal. Hancock also sculpted *Angels of Victory* for the Lorraine American Cemetery in Saint-Avold, France.

8.3   Left on Thirtieth Street. It is safe to ride at this point.

8.5   Right on Walnut Street. *Eltanin* by Bathsheba L. Grossman (1992) is on the corner of Walnut and Thirty-third Streets in front of the Laboratory for Research on the Structure of Matter.

9.0   End at Thirty-fourth and Walnut Street.

🦅 *EAGLE* BY ADOLPH ALEXANDER WEINMAN ON MARKET STREET BRIDGE AT THIRTIETH STREET

ATTRACTIONS IN UNIVERSITY CITY

Arthur Ross Gallery in the Fisher Fine Arts Library, 220 South Thirty-fourth Street, University of Pennsylvania (215) 898-2083, fax (215) 573-2045, Tu–F 10–5, Sa–Su 12–5, http://www.upenn.edu/ARG, free.

Drexel Institute, Thirty-second and Chestnut Streets (215) 895-2000, M–F 8:30–6, Sa 10–12, http://www.drexel.edu, free.

Restaurant School at Walnut Hill College, 4207 Walnut Street (215) 222-4200, Tu–Sa 5:30–10, http://www.therestaurantschool.com, food sales.

University of Pennsylvania Museum of Archaeology and Anthropology, Thirty-third and Spruce Streets (215) 898-4001, Tu–Sa 10–4:30, Su 1–5, http://www.museum.upenn.edu, admission.

Woodlands Cemetery, 4000 Woodland Avenue (215) 386-2181, cemetery M–Th 9–5; mansion M–Th 10–3, free.

For Further Reading

The information in this book comes from many sources. A number of organizations have their own web sites, which I consulted whenever possible. On line, I also consulted *Encyclopedia Britannica* and *American National Biography*, both of which are available by subscription. I viewed the online tour of the city created by the Independence Hall Association at ushistory.org, and I searched the city's web sites at phila.gov and gophila.com, all of which are free to the public.

Published works I read include:

Augustine, Betsy. *Philadelphia's Magic Gardens.* Philadelphia: Open Eyes Books, 1999.

Avery, Ron. *A Concise History of Philadelphia.* Philadelphia: Otis Books, 1999.

Bach, Penny Balkin. *Public Art in Philadelphia.* Philadelphia: Temple University Press, 1992.

Colimore, Edward. *The Philadelphia Inquirer's Guide to Historic Philadelphia.* Philadelphia: Camino Books, 2001.

Morrone, Francis. *An Architectural Guidebook to Philadelphia.* Layton, Utah: Gibbs-Smith, 1999.

Moss, Roger W. *Historic Houses of Philadelphia: A Tour of the Region's Museum Homes.* With photographs by Tom Crane. Philadelphia: University of Pennsylvania Press, 1997.

Philadelphia Architecture: A Guide to the City. 2nd ed. Philadelphia: Foundation for Architecture, 1994.